# HISTORY OF UNION GOSPEL MISSION
## OF TARRANT COUNTY

# HISTORY OF UNION GOSPEL MISSION OF TARRANT COUNTY

*Friends of Union Gospel Mission*

TCU Press
Fort Worth, Texas

Library of Congress Cataloging-in-Publication Data

Names: Union Gospel Mission of Tarrant County. Friends, author.
Title: History of Union Gospel Mission of Tarrant County / Friends of Union Gospel Mission of
        Tarrant County.
Description: Fort Worth, Texas : TCU Press, 2015.
Identifiers: LCCN 2015023153 | ISBN 9780875656090 (alk. paper)
Subjects: LCSH: Union Gospel Mission of Tarrant County--History. | Union Gospel Mission of
        Tarrant County--Biography. | Tarrant County (Tex.)--Church history. | Church work with
        the homeless--Texas--Tarrant County--History.
Classification: LCC BV2806.T37 H57 2015 | DDC 266/.022097645315--dc23
LC record available at http://lccn.loc.gov/2015023153

TCU Press
TCU Box 298300
Fort Worth, Texas 76129
817.257.7822
www.prs.tcu.edu
To order books: 1.800.826.8911

*Cover and text design by fusion29*
*www.fusion29.com*

THIS BOOK IS DEDICATED TO
DON SHISLER
IN APPRECIATION FOR HIS TWENTY YEARS OF
EXEMPLARY SERVICE UNTO OUR LORD JESUS CHRIST
AS PRESIDENT/CEO OF
UNION GOSPEL MISSION OF TARRANT COUNTY

# CONTENTS

# FOREWORD

I AM OVERJOYED THAT THROUGH ALL OF THE HARD WORK PUT IN OVER THE PAST NINE YEARS, THIS BOOK CAN NOW BLESS AND INFORM OUR GENEROUS COMMUNITY OF THE WORK THE LORD HAS ALWAYS BEEN DOING AT UNION GOSPEL MISSION OF TARRANT COUNTY. It is through God's provisions that UGM-TC has been able to operate in serving the "least of these" in Tarrant County since 1888.

I would like to thank the many people that helped make this book a reality, especially Larry Eason and Dr. David Murph for all the dedication and time they put into the making of it. Their thorough research and countless interviews shaped this book into what it is. Thank you to Pat Adams for her generosity in editing and transcribing this volume. I also want to express sincere thanks to Tom Stoker for his contribution to the book. His positive spirit and strength in Christ is evident in all things he does. Lastly, I appreciate everyone who agreed to be interviewed and shared their souls so this story could be told.

Over the twenty-one years that I have been at UGM-TC, I have seen the issues of homelessness evolve, the organization go through highs and lows, and I have had the pleasure of watching countless lives transform before my eyes. When I first began working at the mission, I remember having difficulty spreading awareness around the community about the needs of the homeless. People were simply unsure about the ways in which UGM-TC served the homeless. It was not until *Star-Telegram* writer Jeff Guinn began writing about the issue of homelessness more regularly, and Ron and Deborah Hall began getting involved, that the organization started to become more widely known around town. Since then, UGM-TC has remained the community's place. Without the support of wonderful individuals, churches, businesses, foundations, and government leaders, there would be no Union Gospel Mission of Tarrant County.

As the years have gone by, UGM-TC has continually strived to improve and remain innovative in the ways homelessness is approached. Today, UGM-TC provides hope and a chance for a new start to all who enter through its doors. In the secure environment of the six-acre campus, residents participate in programs designed to maximize their potential by developing the skills they need to return to the community as independent, productive members. The trained staff works to build dependable, trustworthy relationships with clients. A holistic approach is taken to address physical, mental, emotional, and spiritual needs. Clients can openly discuss their unique situations, concerns, strengths, and hopes in the space provided by UGM-TC. The programs offered aim to give homeless individuals the greatest chance to develop the skills and self-confidence they need to attain self-sufficiency.

As UGM-TC moves forward, I know we will continue to face challenges, but with quality, affordable low-income housing, continued case management, and spirituality in their lives, I am confident that the residents who move out of the mission will remain on the course of success.

I hope you will enjoy the stories shared in this book as much as I have enjoyed being a part of the mission. Union Gospel Mission of Tarrant County is no doubt God's healthy place to end homelessness, one person at a time.

In Christ,
DON SHISLER
*President/CEO of Union Gospel Mission of Tarrant County*

# INTRODUCTION

Missions to help the poor and the downtrodden, in the name and spirit of Jesus Christ, are as old as the Bible itself. Through the years they have taken various forms, first in the Mediterranean world, then throughout Europe and, from there, around the globe. What is generally considered the first urban rescue mission was founded in Scotland in 1826. Called Glasgow City Mission, it was launched during a difficult, poverty-ridden period in that city. The result of an interdenominational lay movement, it was Bible based, openly proclaiming the saving grace and power of Jesus Christ. Particularly significant, the Glasgow City Mission prefigured many of its successors by creating partnerships with churches and public agencies that enabled it to deliver a wide range of services.[1]

Precursors of the rescue-mission movement appeared in the United States before the Civil War, taking the form of organizations such as the Ladies' Home Missionary Society and Children's Aid Society in New York City. The American Tract Society also oversaw a number of church and private relief efforts. One of these in particular, the Howard Mission and Home for Little Wanderers, founded in the Bowery, was an important step in the development of missions, as more and more religious-based urban missions expanded from distributing literature to feeding and caring for the poor.[2]

The first actual rescue mission in America was founded in 1872 by a fascinating man named Jerry McAuley. Born in 1839, McAuley had grown up in New York City's notorious Fourth Ward, had committed numerous crimes and, by the age of nineteen, was a prisoner at Sing Sing. Pardoned after seven and a half years, he returned to his criminal ways until meeting Alfrederick Hatch, president of the New York Stock Exchange, who was volunteering at the Howard Mission. Hatch took a special interest in McAuley and encouraged him to do something with his life. One day McAuley experienced what he called a vision. "I was working for the Lord down in the Fourth Ward," he said. "I had a house and people were coming in. There was a bath and they came and I washed and cleaned them outside and the Lord cleaned them inside. . . . Before I came out of the vision I was in tears. Then something said to me, 'Would you do that for the Lord if He should call you? Would you do it for Jesus's sake?' I answered, 'Yes, Lord, open the way and I will go!'"[3]

McAuley was soon operating a rescue mission called Helping Hand for Men. Drunk, homeless, penniless men found refuge here, singing, listening to testimonies, and then sleeping on wooden benches or the floor. They came by the thousands. In the first year alone, McAuley's mission served more than 26,000 meals and provided lodging for 5,144 men. At the end of two years, more than 55,000 people had attended its night meetings.[4]

McAuley's model spread fast, as churches in cities across the country started many similar missions. Some were called city missions. Others, labeled gospel halls, fed the homeless and destitute but provided no lodging. The famed Ryman Auditorium in Nashville, long-time home to the Grand Ole Opry, was built as an evangelistic tabernacle. Often the same people from one town founded numerous other missions in various locations. "They sprang up like weeds around different needs," says Steve Berger, who has written extensively on the subject.[5]

These missions reflected clear, strong religious beliefs. While reaching out to feed the hungry and care for the poor, they placed primary emphasis on the power of Jesus Christ to transform individual lives, his power to save, to redeem fallen human beings and make of them new creations. Challenging social structures and conditions was not the highest priority. What mattered was that the Gospel be proclaimed, that individuals receive Jesus into their hearts, turn their lives over to him, and become saved. Immediate, short-term help and life-changing faith confessions were the heart of these efforts.[6]

This approach was well suited to a growing fundamentalist religious climate in America. Belief in Biblical inerrancy, literal interpretation of scripture, the saving power of Jesus's crucifixion and resurrection, a sharp demarcation between good and evil, between who was saved and who was not, was widespread and boldly proclaimed from churches across the land. Rescue missions were not only a natural outgrowth of these beliefs but also a dramatic, public expression of them. Jesus died for the sins of all. No one—the prostitute, the drunk, the thief—no one was beyond the scope of his saving grace. While the body needed food, the soul required even more—to be reclaimed and saved. So, in many ways, missions became outpost saving stations.[7]

This is the story of one of those saving stations that has grown to become an irreplaceable part of a major American city.

# CHAPTER ONE

By the late 1800s, Fort Worth was growing and changing, struggling to shed its frontier image and become a respectable city. Captain B. B. Paddock, publisher of the *Gazette*, was telling his readers that they could visit the river bluff and watch the first St. Louis, Arkansas and Texas Railway locomotive steam into town. "Fort Worth has more miles of railroad track within its corporate limits than any other city in Texas," he boasted. Two new railroads, the Fort Worth and Denver City Railway to the northwest and the Cotton Belt to the northeast, were just opening. Merchandise from New York and other eastern cities was now being shipped to Fort Worth. W. H. Taylor could announce that his store was carrying ginghams, Swiss flouncing, towels, and ladies' slippers from $1.00 to $3.50. New iron bridges were being built, one over the Trinity River, and miles of streetcar tracks were being added to existing lines. Moreover, the city now had seventeen churches, six banks, a new six-story Board of Trade Building, and a population nearing 23,000.[1]

But Fort Worth was still not far from its rowdy roots. Former city marshal Timothy "Longhair Jim" Courtright had recently been gunned down on Main Street by Luke Short, a local gambling kingpin. Hell's Half Acre, a large section of downtown devoted to prostitution, gambling, and saloons, was still going strong, attracting a seedy element and taxing the town's ability to police itself and maintain some sense of order. Still unsolved was what could only be called a crucifixion—the murder of a woman

known simply as Sally who was found nailed to an outhouse behind a dance hall. And although new settlements west of town were draining off some of the rowdier types, the ongoing spread of saloons and dance halls kept the town's law enforcement officials busy. In fact, one night the police rounded up eight men and, with no way to get that many to jail, had to tie them all together and lead the way.[2]

By 1888 the rescue-mission movement had finally reached Fort Worth in the form of Bethel Mission, an enterprise begun by several downtown churches to care for cowboys, prostitutes, drunks, and drifters with nowhere to go but the streets. As was the case with a number of street missions during this period that spent more time helping people than keeping records, its origins are not clearly documented. The mission was launched at Cumberland Presbyterian Church on the northeast corner of Fifth and Taylor Streets but did not stay there long. An 1891 publication cited its location as Fourteenth Street, near Main. The fact that one source calls it Union Bethel Mission hints that even its original name is unclear.[3]

Little survives to tell of Bethel Mission's beginning years. One of the first accounts describes an afternoon, early in the 1890s, when a young man named Charley Byron walked through its door. He had recently arrived from Scotland, bringing with him an unusual talent. Charley was a ventriloquist. He had joined a traveling troupe that performed in theaters across the country, and on this particular evening was walking along a Fort Worth sidewalk on his way to the Majestic Theater for one more show. Suddenly he heard the sounds of Gospel music trumpeted by a small brass band emerging from a nearby building. Curious, he stepped inside.[4]

Charley was in for a surprise, because that door was not only the entry to the mission but also to a new life. For one thing, he was about to meet Ashley Attwell, the woman who would become his wife. A Presbyterian church volunteer, she had been engaged to a Methodist missionary serving in China. From Galveston she traveled by ship to New York City to marry him, only to discover upon arrival that he had died. She returned to Fort Worth and happened to be volunteering at the mission the evening Charley wandered in. Charley never made it to the theater that night, or any future night. Transformed and energized by the mission's message of Jesus Christ's saving grace, he left for Chicago to enroll in the Moody Bible Institute, one of the best-known Bible schools in the nation, founded by famed evangelist Dwight L. Moody. After finishing his studies and returning to Fort Worth, he and Ashley were married.[5]

Little is known of Bethel Mission in the waning years of the nineteenth century. Apparently, in 1891, a man named Hodges was superintendent. That same year, the monthly bulletin of Fort Worth's new Young Men's Christian Association, referring to the venture as Union Bethel Mission, announced that it was holding services nightly at its new rooms on Main Street, between Fourteenth and Fifteenth, and that "the spirit of the Master is most surely with the Bethel workers."[6]

Apparently Charley Byron quickly became a key figure at the mission. In 1893 he is mentioned as "missionary in charge of the Bethel Mission," and also as a participant in a highly publicized police incident. It revolved around the minister of Broadway Baptist Church, Dr. A. E. Baten. Convinced that some aldermen and policemen were taking payments to favor certain saloons and houses of prostitution in Hell's Half Acre, Baten donned a disguise and, with Charley Byron in tow, went to see for himself.[7]

But there was a problem. Although Baten made these charges from the pulpit of Broadway Baptist Church, he refused to pursue them. He even prepared an affidavit outlining the charges but would not appear before the city council committee formed to oversee police conduct. A few people responded to the committee's call for witnesses, but could not provide enough information to be helpful.[8]

Enter Charley Byron. As Baten's story came under suspicion and even attack, Byron appeared before the council committee and then issued a statement saying: "I am perfectly willing to substantiate everything I told the committee . . . and will tell the names of the places we visited so far as I can remember them." He added: "My only desire is to tell the absolute truth regarding this whole matter." But first he wanted to meet with the directors of the mission. His actions would be governed by their wishes.[9]

The directors must have opposed another committee appearance by Byron and recommended, instead, that he issue a statement. Accordingly, Byron wrote and handed to a reporter a statement saying, among other things, "What I have said by affidavit and before the police committee I can substantiate fully. . . ." After claiming that he and Baten visited two gambling houses, he said, "We also visited some, but not all by any means, of the houses of ill repute in the acre, and the Variety Theater." He wanted it known that he and Baten had done this in "a respectable way." He claimed that he frequently saw police in saloons and admitted that he saw one officer on the night of his visit but did not want to judge whether or not applicable laws were being enforced. He made no additional reference to Baten's disguise and closed on a serious note about himself: "My work is to save men from all evil resorts, which I try in my humble way to do. What I have said by affidavit and not by hearsay or report is reliable." When requested to furnish more details to the newspaper, Byron said that after carefully consulting with the "managers of the mission," the above statement was as far as he was prepared to go.[10]

So Baten's charges went nowhere. Though he had leveled his accusations from the pulpit, even naming names, and was supported by Charley Byron, his refusal to appear before the council committee ensured that outcome. As a result, the council went on the offensive and accused those making the charges of actually trying to thwart the investigation. Its report concluded with a statement declaring that the police officers had been fully exonerated and that the charges in every case had been disproved.[11]

By the close of 1893, Charley Byron had become superintendent of a new Bethel Mission in Denison. This was a reflection of his and the mission's success. The Bethel movement had done so well in Fort Worth that a second mission was opened downtown and a new one launched in Denison. The location was no accident. Railroads had come to Denison early as they pushed southward toward Fort Worth and Dallas. It had become a significant connecting point and, consequently, a haven for the homeless and for people seeking work. In one night alone, the Denison mission recorded one hundred conversions. Those promoting Bethel missions claimed, "They are among the most successful agencies for the reformation of the fallen," and they were already planning the next one for Galveston.[12]

By this time, a man named L. M. Cooper had become superintendent of Fort Worth's Bethel Mission, which was showing impressive results. In one month—January 1894—the Sunday night meetings drew four hundred to five hundred people. More than five thousand people had attended services during that month, and the Sunday school claimed an attendance of approximately seven hundred children. In addition, Superintendent Cooper, after encouraging Fort Worth citizens to donate books, had created free reading rooms where he set up his office and encouraged men who sought shelter on cold nights to read and write there.[13]

Cooper was also good at enlisting help and recruited ministers from several backgrounds. While Cooper oversaw services at Bethel Mission, Rev. W.P. Wilson, a Methodist, conducted services at Holland's Variety Theater on Sunday nights, reaching some 150 men. In addition to Reverend Wilson, he brought aboard Reverend Sensibough, another Methodist; Reverend Dr. Bailey, a Baptist; Reverend Martin, a Presbyterian; Reverend H. Cassel, an Episcopalian; and numerous volunteers from their congregations. In addition, he planned a series of revival services to be led by various pastors from across the city, each church to be responsible for one week of meetings. True to its roots, Bethel Mission continued to be an ecumenical venture.[14]

It was intentionally nonsectarian. In fact, all Bethel missions, while working closely with evangelical churches, were careful not to identify with any one denomination or faction. In the words of L. M. Cooper, "It is the uniform practice of all Bethel missions to urge upon their converts the utter necessity of unity with some branch of the evangelical church," but as to which church, that was to be left to the discretion of the convert. "The Bethel Mission has heretofore, does now and will forever decline to be dominated and controlled by sectarianism. Its object," Cooper said, "is to glorify God and to save men and women. It has the seal of God upon it and it will take more than the egotistical cant of any man or sect of men to undo the things that God has done."[15]

The mission was holding services in several locations, finding or creating accommodations as needed. In October 1894, the mission erected a large tent on Eleventh Street, between Main and Houston, where it hosted the state convention of the Highways and Hedges Ministry, an organization supporting various rescue mission efforts. To the tent came delegates from Dallas, Abilene, El Paso, Denison, Houston, and other Texas cities. Afterward the tent was used for Bethel-sponsored revival meetings, which facilitated not only conversions but also, on one evening, the theft of a buggy and phaeton from J. S. Jones, an attendee. Several people claimed to have seen a man and woman drive it off. Other services were held outdoors on street corners. The most publicized was led by Rev. L. O. Bryan, called the "clown preacher," who had been converted at the mission while in Fort Worth with the Sells Brothers Circus four years earlier.[16]

As 1897 dawned, a reporter for the *Fort Worth Record* wrote a telling account of a Sunday evening at the mission's main location, on Ninth and Main. The room was nearly full a half hour before the meeting began. The assemblage was "largely made up of men, principally mechanics and laboring men, with a sprinkling of the tough element, which is generally, by some inexplicable reason, always represented in this particular class of sinners." Following a sermon about the prodigal son's return, seven men came forward asking to be prayed for. Among them were several described as having "the stride and swing of the bowery tough," but "in their faces could be seen an humble and earnest look." The meeting closed with the superintendent, P. F. Morgan, reminding those present that the mission depended entirely on private donations and that current finances were dangerously low.[17]

Despite its shaky financial condition, Bethel Mission was reaching a lot of people. In the span of only one month, it recorded an attendance of five thousand, as well as twenty-two conversions and 180 people requesting prayers. Its work went well beyond preaching, however. One day a distraught mother, unable to care for her three-month-old child, left it on the counter of a Main Street restaurant saying, "I can't take care of it and myself, too." Before anyone realized what was happening, she kissed the baby, turned, and disappeared into the street. The shocked restaurant owner, not knowing what else to do, took the child home with her overnight, made an improvised cradle, and brought the baby back to the restaurant the next morning. A few moments later, the mother, distraught, appeared, hugged and kissed her baby, and said what she needed most was a job that would enable her to care for the child.

Bethel Mission quickly entered the picture. The ladies of the mission found employment for the mother at a local hotel restaurant. These women solicited donations to supplement the hotel's low wages, and together the funds were enough for the mother to keep and care for her child. Both the mission and the restaurant continued to support the mother who had appeared at their doorsteps.[18]

It may come as a surprise that preachers at Bethel included women. In March 1897, a woman by the name of Rogers drew large crowds to the mission to hear her sermons. Hailing from Greenville, Texas, she apparently had built a strong reputation as an eloquent, effective preacher. Following her sermons, it was not uncommon for the altar rail to be lined with people seeking prayer, and a number of conversions were recorded. During this same period, Mrs. C. A. Drake, who bore the title "city missionary," also preached at the mission. Obviously, occupying a pulpit at the mission was not solely a male entitlement.[19]

In fact, one of the ways the mission attracted attention was by announcing colorful speakers. In addition to L.O. Bryan, identified as a "converted clown" in the mission's promotions for its Sunday night services, there was Felix Crow, who appeared in the newspaper under the headline "A Converted Water Hauler Will Preach Tonight." Crow had been converted at a mission meeting some years earlier, and had been sent by Bethel Mission to Kentucky to study for the ministry. Now returned to begin his work, Reverend Crow encouraged all his old friends to come, "particularly the water haulers of Fort Worth."[20]

In April 1897, the mission issued an impressive report for the first three months of the year. It recorded 12,015 in attendance, ninety-two conversions, 386 persons desiring to become Christians, 112 jail services, and sixty street services. In addition, the mission had provided lodging for 390 people and served meals to 375. All this had been accomplished at a cost of $175.55. "We have distributed food, old clothing, etc., among the poor and have found employment for many who were in need, both men and women," said Superintendent Morgan. "We invite all who feel interested in city mission work to call and see us at any time."[21]

By July of 1897, the same Mrs. Drake who had recently preached at Bethel Mission was now its superintendent. That same month she issued an encouraging statement saying: "Good meetings, good attendance and much interest is manifested at this place. Plenty of ice water and fans are furnished. Come one and all." She announced Thursday afternoon Bible readings as well as a children's Sunday school. "Dear worker," she pleaded, "Let us gather up the little ones that are not attending Sunday school and teach them the way of life. If we capture the lambs, the sheep will follow." In addition to these activities, the mission hosted meetings of the Loyal Temperance Legion, one of the several organizations promoting the growing temperance movement.[22]

Despite its success, Bethel Mission was about to experience significant change. The first signs were evident in an October 1897 *Fort Worth Register* story announcing that a meeting of mission workers would soon be held to elect a new

superintendent, and that the current board of trustees would resign and a new one would be elected. Then an announcement came that Drake would be leaving to lead a Dallas mission, and a Mr. Jacques would be the new Bethel superintendent. Mrs. C. W. Byron (Charley's wife), Mrs. Ingram, Mrs. Belle Campbell, and Miss Rebecca Collins were named as new trustees. This was followed by an explanation of the changes and word that controversy had bred them. In an October 1897 issue of the *Fort Worth Register*, evangelist R. K. Richardson described the problems. "The holiness people of Fort Worth," he claimed, "have felt led for some time to start a mission where the doctrine of sanctification, as a second work of grace, can be preached, whereby believers are enabled to enjoy in this life a conscious 'freedom from sin.'" After sharing more details of this doctrine, Richardson claimed that Bethel Mission had "lost her usefulness on account of internal dissention," one faction focusing on "loaves and fishes," another on the "One Man" doctrine, and both opposed to Sister C. A. Drake.[23]

As a result, Richardson was announcing the creation of a new mission and announcing that Sister Drake, rather than going to Dallas, would be leading this new effort. It would be located at 1110 Main Street, with services every night. Preachers would come from various denominations, the only requirement being their willingness to declare the "whole counsel of God." The "new mission," said Richardson rather disingenuously, "is not started in opposition to the Bethel Mission, which we wish Godspeed, but we feel led of God to give Fort Worth a mission where sinners can be saved and believers sanctified." Apparently, he believed Bethel could do neither.

# CHAPTER TWO

By the close of the century the same Charley Byron whose curiosity had led him through the Bethel Mission door a few years earlier had become its superintendent. In newspaper notices he was announcing Sunday evening Gospel services, saying simply: "Come to a good meeting." By now Charley had become more than a ventriloquist and Bible-school graduate; he was also a songwriter. In fact, so moved was he by his conversion to Christ at the mission, he wrote a seven-verse gospel hymn entitled "Diamonds in the Rough" to describe the experience. It began:

> While walking out one evening,
>    Not knowing where to go,
> And just to pass the lone hours
>    Before we held the show,
> The Bethel Mission Band pass'd,
>    All singing with their might,
> And gave my heart to Jesus
>    And left the show that night.

And continued....

> I used to dance the polka,
>    The schottische and the waltz,
> I also loved the theater,
>    Its glitter vain and false.
> But Jesus when he found me,
>    He found me very tough,
> But praise the Lord, he saved me,
>    I'm a diamond in the rough.

Charley must not have been superintendent long, because he also spent time as a Methodist circuit rider preaching to cowboys on the West Texas range shortly before his death of kidney disease, in 1905, at the age of forty-two.[1]

But Charley Byron had ushered Bethel Mission into a new century and a new era in the life of Fort Worth. Though saloons were still numerous—the White Elephant on Main Street being the most colorful—and many downtown buildings were in sad repair, quiet residential neighborhoods were growing fast. In fact, the city's population now exceeded twenty-six thousand. The first automobiles were sputtering along its newly bricked and paved streets. Moreover, both Swift and Armour were announcing plans to build large packinghouses in Fort Worth, major economic news. By 1905, Fort Worth's population had jumped to forty-two thousand, Main Street was paved all the way from the courthouse to the T&P station, and Houston Street was paved from Weatherford to Tenth Street.[2]

Bethel Mission, however, was not faring as well as the city. While still serving its original purpose, proclaiming the saving power of Jesus Christ and ministering to those in need, its organizational structure and support were floundering. The fact that it was housed in rented quarters and bounced from one location to another had not helped. There had been no board of directors—only a loose, ever-changing group of well-meaning volunteers. Churches must have found the mission easy to overlook in their budgeting. Some of its most optimistic backers had even reached the point of wondering if Bethel Mission would survive. That uncertainty was about to change.

The year 1909 would be critical. On June 17,

concerned about its declining state, a number of Fort Worth pastors and others interested in evangelistic work met at First Methodist Church to reorganize Bethel Mission and give it a fresh start. Several ministers delivered impassioned addresses, among them Rev. H. W. Matthews, Rev. W. J. Caldwell, and a Dr. Dozier. Also speaking was evangelist Newton McClurkin of Los Angeles, who shared his experience with successful missions on the West Coast. By the end of the meeting, an organizational plan was presented and the first board of directors selected. William Reeves was elected president, E. J. White vice president, Warren Collins secretary, and W. D. Thomas treasurer. They presided over a board composed of B. H. Getz, Dr. J. H. Horne, LeRoy Smith, G. H. Connell, W. E. Williams, H. M. Bradley, and R. F. Dixon. "No creed but Christ; no law but love" was the motto chosen to guide their work. A local reporter noted, "All present entered into the spirit of the work with a zest that bespeaks well for the future of the movement."[3]

One of the most noteworthy members of this group was Warren Collins. His wife, Delia, had been a mission founder, and for more than a quarter of a century he would serve as its recording secretary and primary booster. Owner of the Collins Art Company, he was a generous Fort Worth benefactor devoted to evangelistic work, who helped lead the mission through its turbulent early twentieth-century years.[4]

The new organization and enthusiasm must have been just what the mission needed, for at the end of the next year, its superintendent, Ira Eldridge, issued an encouraging first annual report. The numbers were heartening: 375 mission meetings, 450 shop, jail, and street services, two hundred services conducted at the mission by pastors, seven hundred free meals served, 5,525 men sheltered in the mission "rooming department," and seven hundred conversions. Almost ten thousand men had come seeking employment. Average at-

tendance at nightly meetings was eighty-five, with a total of some 31,875 people attending. "Hundreds have been reached on the streets with the Gospel Wagon and in the shops and jail services and by the house-to-house visiting committee, composed of the Ladies Home Missionary League," the report boasted. The mission showed an income of $4,005 and expenses of $4,656—of which $2,400 was spent for rent at its 1502 Main Street quarters.

By now, more than structure and reporting were changing. At some point during this period Bethel Mission became Union Gospel Mission. And leadership was also in transition. In 1910, the directors made what would become a mission-changing decision—choosing Sam Mayfield as superintendent. Born in Kentucky shortly after the Civil War, Sam worked for the Katy Railroad, and for the rest of his life, remembered the exact day of his conversion to Jesus Christ—June 30, 1890. Five years later he committed his life to full-time Christian service and came to Denison, Texas, to supervise the local Young Men's Christian Association. In 1906 he moved to Decatur, Illinois, where he had been appointed general secretary of the railroad YMCA, and four years later was in Fort Worth to begin what would become his life's work.[6]

The directors made a good choice. A short, stocky, energetic man, Sam Mayfield assumed the leadership role at a propitious time in the life of Union Gospel Mission—when its new structure and mission had just been formulated and enthusiasm was high. What was needed was a leader, and from every indication, Sam was just that. He would lead the mission for almost three decades and dramatically increase the scope of its ministry.[7] During the first years of Mayfield's leadership, the mission seemed to have stabilized and had made itself well known. Sam invited everyone from local ministers to laypersons and civic leaders to lead the 9:00 a.m. and 3:30 p.m. services in the meeting hall. He especially relied on the administration, faculty, and students at Southwestern Baptist Theological Seminary in Fort Worth to fill his roster of speakers. All in all, it was quite a cast. On a November Sunday morning in 1913, for example, S. D. Hartman, a probation officer, spoke to policemen at the early service, and a policeman named Coffey sang. Later that same day, Charles Murdell, a young man known as the boy evangelist of Dallas, spoke to such a large crowd that 150 people had to stand outside. His topic: "The Highest Price Ever Paid for a Hair Cut." The very next week, joined by an orchestra and forty-voice choir, he was back, preaching to one of the largest crowds ever to gather at the mission. At the close of the service, twenty-five people requested prayer and were converted to Jesus Christ.

By the end of November 1913, the mission had recorded ninety conversions for the month. At the very heart of the mission's ministry, these conversions were its primary reason for being. The process was not complicated. Those seeking conversion were asked to acknowledge the error of their ways, to ask forgiveness, and to invite Jesus to enter their hearts and help them begin a new life in Christ. From its early days the mission considered these conversions to be critical, and counted and included them in annual reports.

Although conversions were increasing, the mission's budget was not. In 1914, its total income was $4,006.18, just $1.58 more than in 1910. While a majority of this money came from local churches, items such as tag days, miscellaneous stocks, and a rummage sale accounted for most of the rest. On the disbursement side, the largest expenses were $1,490 for rent and $1,202 to Sam Mayfield.

During the next two years, as war first threatened Europe and then enveloped most of it, Mayfield invited ministers and laypersons of various backgrounds from across the city to preach at the mission's Sunday services. In March 1914, George E. Nies, a railroad official

who would give much of his time to the mission, spoke on the topic "Right Side Up," which followed a morning message by the Reverend J. F. Singleton on the text, "He that covers his sin shall not prosper, but he that confesseth shall have mercy." That fall Judge John Thompson of Stephenville spoke about "What the Blind Man Saw," claiming that "many persons with good eyesight are blinded by sin." Six conversions followed his message.

The following year, Reverend F. E. Gordon of St. Paul's Methodist Church was speaking to a crowded mission hall about "True Manhood Tested" and "A Lucky Strike," while mission supporter George Nies, week after week, was delivering Sunday afternoon messages on topics such as "Life's Highway to Heaven" and "Is Christianity a Failure?" A number of conversions, all duly recorded, concluded each service. And so it went through 1915, with crowds packing the mission hall to hear messages that focused on reclaiming lives. In fact, by the end of the year, the small quarters had become so packed that Sam Mayfield relocated the mission to a larger building one block away, at 1404 Main Street.

As 1916 dawned, the move to new quarters was not the only development making news. The perpetrator of one of the most publicized murders in recent Tarrant County history was attending mission services and drawing attention to them. Ike Knight had killed his son-in-law and then, while resisting arrest, wounded two police officers, one a future Fort Worth police chief, O. R. Montgomery. Knight was first sentenced to death, then, in a second trial, drew seventy-five years in the penitentiary and finally, in still another trial, had his sentence reduced to five years. While an appeal for this sentence was pending, he was arrested on a bigamy charge. He had served only twenty-one months of his five-year term when, on Christmas Day, 1915, Texas governor James E. Ferguson pardoned him. The bigamy charge was later dropped.[8]

Following his pardon, one of the first places Knight visited was Union Gospel Mission. Night after night he came, testifying that he had become a reformed person, that he had been conducting evangelistic work in prison and had converted at least two men. This, he claimed, had an impact on many others. Eyes were riveted on Knight as he declared: "I think I see a chance to do some good with the rest of my life. I'm going to try to do it." He told the crowd that he intended to live "an upright life."[9]

New Year's Day was remarkable. In addition to hearing Knight, in his third appearance at the mission, describe his changed ways, several hundred people also watched Sam Mayfield and his assistants burn seventeen bottles of whiskey in the gutter in front of the mission's new headquarters. They listened to Rev. D. V. Edwards, pastor of College Avenue Baptist Church, deliver a message that led to six conversions. And Mayfield still had his New Year's resolutions to share. They included holding five hundred services in the mission, in railroad stations, jails, and other locations during 1916; converting twelve hundred people; and sending a thousand new members to area churches. "There are some sixty-five thousand persons in Fort Worth now who do not attend church," he claimed, "and I believe there are at least ten thousand who have been members of churches in other cities but who have not put in their letters here." Reaching these people, he announced, would be a primary mission goal.[10]

A few days later, Union Gospel Mission was officially incorporated. Its purpose would be "to support all maintenance of a gospel mission." By the end of January, Mayfield had announced a new financial campaign to support the mission's work for another year. Figuring that it cost about fifteen dollars a day to run the mission, he asked religious and business leaders, as well as all Fort Worth citizens, to pay expenses for at least one day. Each donor would be given a stock certificate for every fifteen dollars committed. Since the corporation listed no capital, obviously no dividends would be paid. "The work can better be taken care of with a $5,000 budget," he said, "but positively cannot be done on less than $4,500."[11]

Mayfield bolstered his case with a positive report, showing 750 conversions and more than fifty-five thousand in attendance the preceding year. Moreover, for January alone, he reported seventy-six conversions, fifty-one religious services attended by 5,600 persons, 215 requests for prayer, and 380 lunches served to the hungry. Just as impressive was the mission's ministry at the county jail. Five hundred and seventeen people had attended fifteen religious services. And what Mayfield considered especially important was the fact that twenty individuals who had converted at the mission had joined various churches in the city during the month. Judge R. D. Gage, president of the mission board and leader of the campaign, said it well: "Let the doubter ask his own pastor and he will learn that more than a baker's dozen . . . have become active members through the medium of this religious force."[12]

Several talented, committed men stepped forward to promote the campaign. Among them was George Nies, surely one of the strongest leaders in this era of Union Gospel Mission's life. Manager of the Texas and Pacific Railway telegraph relay office, Nies was not only a mission board member, he was also a frequent speaker at its many services—one of its most recognizable names and faces. He made the case that the mission deserved support because, among its many notable achievements, the mission received visitors from all over the nation who were unlikely ever to enter a church but heard the gospel preached in the mission hall. Union Gospel Mission's scope, he claimed, went far beyond Fort Worth: it was nationwide and deserved to be placed on a solid financial footing.

Joining Nies was Rev. Forrest Smith, pastor of Broadway Baptist Church. Smith called the mission one of the "live religious forces" of Fort Worth, attracting many people who did not attend church. "They hear the gospel preached," he said. "They are convicted of sin, of righteousness and of judgment and then are converted and many of them join churches and make faithful servants of God." In his opinion, Sam Mayfield was just the right person to lead the mission and run the campaign.[13]

This campaign, like many others to come, would reflect the mission's close connection to the Texas and Pacific Railway. One strong link was George Nies. Another was simple proximity: the railway terminal was across the street from the mission, bringing workers and all kinds of people, locals and nonlocals alike, to the mission every day. But one of the strongest connections was in the person of John L. Lancaster. In 1916, during some tough times, the Texas and Pacific Railway Company went into receivership, and Lancaster was brought in as one of the court-appointed receivers. He would become president of the railroad, as well as a generous supporter of the mission.[14]

Sam Mayfield, who seemed to have an inexhaustible supply of ideas, identified with the railroad workers and their needs. While the annual campaign was still in progress, he announced a plan to collect fifty thousand magazines to be distributed among ten thousand section hands who spent lonely nights and Sundays in railroad camps near Fort Worth. Citizens were urged to search closets, basements, and attics, to collect every magazine they could find, and then contact the mission, which would send a wagon to pick them up. Mayfield would begin distributing them as soon as he had collected twenty-five thousand. "Our sole aim is to help the railroad men spend their evenings pleasantly," he said. "At least six men are at every section house, and I know from my experience with railroad men that the evening

hours sometimes drag slowly for them." In April, continuing his commitment to the railroad, Mayfield hosted the second annual Railroad Day, attended by sixty men representing every railroad in the city. Officials of all Texas railroads were invited, including J. H. Elliott of Dallas, superintendent of the Texas and Pacific, and J. W. Everman of Tyler, general manager of the Cotton Belt.[15]

Sam did not hesitate to become involved in what he considered moral issues affecting Fort Worth. Movies were a good example. On February 14, 1916, the city commission debated a proposal to allow movie theaters to open on Sundays after 2:00 p.m. Mayor E. T. Tyra opposed it, as did Mayfield, who contributed to the meeting, becoming boisterous and almost out of control. F. W. Axtell opened the meeting with a denunciation of the resolution, which he labeled a desecration of the Sabbath. To his statement "If you are looking for peace and harmony, this is a poor way of getting it," Mayfield shouted "Amen!" Then, when Axtell tried to keep talking, Mayor Tyra ordered him to sit down. Axtell continued: "This will follow you to your grave. Stand up and be men." Sam stood up and again shouted "Amen!"[16]

On and on the debate raged, with the closing of saloons and even Hell's Half Acre being injected into the arguments. Finally, as the shouting subsided, it was time to vote. The issue: whether to call a special election to let citizens decide the matter. Mayor Tyra was the lone commissioner who opposed this move. Above the cheers and applause that followed the mayor's vote, Sam could be heard shouting, "We are for you!"[17]

Sam Mayfield, full of ideas and energy and blessed with impressive vision, lived by a strict personal code. Apparently, profanity violated it. On an evening shortly before Railroad Day, as he stepped into an office in the Fort Worth Electric Light and Power Company to distribute a Union Gospel Mission circular, he was approached by a moving-picture operator who unleashed a stream of profanity at him. Although Mayfield told a policeman to arrest the man and charge him with abusive language, he said if he received an apology, he would not file charges against him. The episode clearly puzzled Mayfield. "I never saw you before. I don't know why you commenced cursing," Mayfield told him at police headquarters. Though obviously bothered by this, upon later learning that the man was the son of one of his close friends, Mayfield decided to drop the matter.[18]

By 1916 it had become apparent that the move to 1404 Main Street had not solved the mission's space problems. Something had to be done, and in May, major plans were unveiled. The *Fort Worth Star-Telegram* announced that "Twenty-four representative men of Fort Worth who constitute the board of directors of Union Gospel Mission of Tarrant County decided that the hour had come for action in order that the mission should have a permanent home, its work broadened and the institution placed on a stable financial foundation." Calling the present quarters cramped and inadequate, the article gave readers a good summary of the mission's ministry: "Wanderers who have strayed beyond the gate of the Shepherd are reclaimed by Union Gospel Mission by the thousands, restoring to society an army of workers who had temporarily fallen by the wayside."[19]

The directors had their eyes on a three-story stone building at Fourteenth and Main streets owned by John Shelton of Amarillo. Several years earlier he had bought the building for $83,500. At the invitation of the mission's directors, Shelton came to Fort Worth, and after hearing their plans, offered the building to them for the same price he had paid for it. The obvious challenge was finding a way to raise that much money. Determined not to lose this opportunity, the directors acted quickly. Led by their president, Dr. R. H. Gough, they began by pledging $2,000 of their own money and then announced a campaign to raise the rest.[20]

And what a campaign this was to be! Described as "aggressive and even the high-pressure type," it would be launched during the first week of June. Two hundred Fort Worth men and women would be encouraged to lead a short, high-intensity effort spanning only ten business days. Sundays, of course, were to be excluded. A local writer, describing the mission on the eve of its ambitious campaign, called it "one of the most unique institutions of a religious nature in the Southwest," and claimed that "many men who had lost hold on society have entered its doors as failures and gone out to make a new start in life." He went so far as to say that a number of prominent citizens of Fort Worth and other cities call the mission the "turning point" in their lives.[21]

One of the strongest cases to find a permanent home for the mission was made by Associate Justice Buck of the Second Court of Civil Appeals:

A downtown mission whose open doors welcome the stranger and the straggler, the seeker and the sinner, is a Christian necessity for any great city. It becomes an open door harbor for any storm-driven, wind-tossed derelict, a haven within whose inviting protection he has full help and hope, and there find strength and courage to continue his voyage under new power and with another compass. . . . A mission fills a place in the religious activities of a city that the church doesn't and perhaps in the nature of things, can't fill. The transient, the idler, the loafer, the merely curious minded must be reached, his wavering attention fixed, and his feeble purpose to reform individually encouraged and strengthened. Therefore, methods entirely different from those proper and effective in city churches are here to be employed. . . . I have studied the work done by Union Gospel Mission, under Superintendent Mayfield, and feel sure much good is being accomplished, that many a downcast has been uplifted, many a hopeless wanderer shown the error of his ways and placed on the right path, and many a soul saved from ruin and despair. I have known of a number of instances where men were arrested from what seemed to be the final downgrade plunge.

I hope the time will soon come when this great interdenominational work will be housed under a roof of its own, where the moneyless may find material assistance, the idle may find profitable labor, and the despairing may realize that the human heart is still kind and still willing to aid the needy brother in his distress. This is the kind of religion in which we all must believe, the kind that appeals with strongest force to those whose hearts are without hope and whose lives are without joy.

Later that year, mission leaders received sad news. Col. Paul Waples, one of the mission's most vocal and generous supporters, was killed when his automobile collided with an Interurban trolley car. His driver, heeding Colonel Waples's shout to stop, unfortunately brought the car to a halt on the trolley tracks. President of Waples-Platter Grocery Company and chairman of Wortham-Carter Publishing Company, which published the *Star-Telegram*, Colonel Waples had been a mainstay of Union Gospel Mission of Tarrant County. He had told its story to others and given liberally of his resources. His absence would obviously be felt.[22]

The most ominous news, however, was the First World War raging in Europe. In April of 1917, President Woodrow Wilson, his hand forced by German provocation, asked Congress for a declaration of war, and the United States quickly became involved. In Fort Worth, recruiting began in earnest. Posters imitating those of George Washington's Continental Army were prominently displayed around town, and the first recruits began signing up. Assistant Secretary of Agriculture Carl Vrooman came to Fort Worth to plead for increased production of food crops, declaring that, because of the possible disruption of normal transportation, the South must be able to feed itself. That same week a large patriotic parade made its way through downtown. Enthusiasm for the war effort was high.[23]

# CHAPTER THREE

The war had a quick and dramatic impact on Fort Worth. In June 1917, an army commission arrived to search for a location to build a large training facility. By July, Camp Bowie, named for Alamo defender James Bowie, was under construction. Three miles west of downtown, encompassing 2,186 acres, the camp had as its primary purpose the training of the Thirty-Sixth Infantry Division. By war's end, it would train more than 100,000 men and affect not only Fort Worth in general but also Union Gospel Mission of Tarrant County.

As Fort Worth and the nation mobilized for war, the mission moved into its recently acquired, three-story building. Sam Mayfield, as busy as ever, began seeking employment opportunities for people coming in off the street. In August, in addition to his superintendent duties, he had created and become manager of the Free Employment Bureau, an organization formed to match workers with jobs. Even so, he was unable to fill the demand for labor. By mid-October, the Rock Island Line needed seventy-four workers and the Cotton Belt fifty. Sam was able to provide only fifteen qualified men, all of whom went to the Cotton Belt. But overall, the new employment bureau was succeeding. In only two months it found employment for 994 laborers, some with the railroad and others on nearby farms.[1]

That year, as Christmas approached and a professor at Southwestern Baptist Theological Seminary preached at the mission about Christ coming into the world to save sinners, Sam Mayfield was making plans. Seventy-five well-stocked baskets would be distributed to families in need, and on Christmas night, men without jobs and those he called "strangers" would be invited to a dinner in the mission hall. He knew to prepare for at least five hundred.[2]

The next year would be busy and productive. In February 1918, the mission hosted a lunch at the YMCA for the pastors and boards of directors of a number of Fort Worth churches. The object was to involve more congregations in the service of the mission. Jim Goodheart of Denton, long involved in mission work, was the principal speaker, urging those present to become more involved with the mission and to increase the number of churches supporting it. Describing a gospel mission as a "church in overalls," Goodheart reminded his audience that these outposts reach a class of people who hesitate to enter a church because of "financial embarrassment."[3]

Reminders of the war were never far away. Dr. James Francis, pastor of Los Angeles's First Baptist Church, was in town not only to address local pastors, but also for a series of lectures at Camp Bowie. Sunday after Sunday, ministers preached to large crowds at the mission hall, with special entertainment often provided for the soldiers.[4]

Those large crowds and powerful evangelical preaching also led to increased conversions, which were recorded and announced weekly. For instance, on February 17, following a sermon on the prodigal son, eleven conversions were reported, making a three-week total of ninety-five. In mid-March, Dr. Lee Scarborough, president of the Baptist seminary, delivered a sermon on the need for salvation that led to ten conversions. That brought the March total to fifty-seven. In June, a service led by the pastor of the Tabernacle Church produced eleven conversions, eight of whom were soldiers, and a late-July service brought that month's number to 110.[5]

But despite the large crowds and impressive conversion numbers, money was still owed on the purchase price of the new building. Accordingly, in August, the mission's board announced that a $29,000 campaign would be launched on September 11. This undertaking had as its goal not only to pay off a note still outstanding, but also to renovate and remodel some upstairs areas. Over the chapel a large, fully equipped reading and writing room would be created. In addition, thirty-six private bedrooms and a number of new showers were to be provided.[6]

During this period, Camp Bowie and the Thirty-Sixth Infantry Division figured large in the mission's life. Soldiers from the camp showed up in numbers to attend the mission's Sunday services. In October 1918, as the war neared an end, the majority of the large crowds that packed the mission were Camp Bowie soldiers. Even in June of the following year, seven months after the armistice, Thirty-Sixth Infantry soldiers recently returned from overseas comprised the majority of the worshippers at mission services. Two months later Camp Bowie was closed, and the area rapidly became a residential neighborhood.

Meanwhile, the new building was exceeding expectations. It was large enough to accommodate a number of functions. An auditorium for worship services, the office of the Free Employment Bureau, and a dining area were on the main floor. The basement housed not only the heating plant but also lavatory, shower, and tub

facilities as well. Dormitory-style rooms filled the second and third floors. Finally the mission had adequate space in which to operate.[7]

Under Sam Mayfield's leadership the mission continued to thrive. In the fall of 1919, plans were announced to add six more directors, bringing the number to twenty-five business and professional men. Moreover, the building debt was on the way to retirement. Fifty thousand dollars had been paid on the building, $18,000 in 1919 alone, leaving an indebtedness of $33,500. Two $16,000 notes were to be paid within the coming year. In September four more directors were elected, and a five-person advisory board was appointed. That same month Dr. H. E. Stout, president of Texas Woman's College, spoke before the directors, asserting that the mission's ministry compared favorably with larger missions around the country and praised its good work in Fort Worth.[8]

That fall was busy. By October, Mayfield was announcing the mission's sponsorship of fifty services a week during the coming winter and spring. Many of these would be noon meetings in factories and shops. The mission was reaching out to workers where they lived and worked. By November, another financial campaign was underway. Several ten-member teams would be on the streets, trying to sell 30,000 buttons for one dollar apiece. Twenty thousand sold fast; the remaining ten thousand would take a while.[9]

Then it was time to make plans for Christmas. That year the mission would distribute two hundred food baskets to the poor, each costing five dollars and filled to feed a family of five. The job was made easier by two directors' donations of two hundred sacks of flour, one for each basket. In addition, a Christmas dinner was being planned to feed as many as three hundred boys in the mission building. A number of women from local churches volunteered to help.

This bountiful Christmas was followed by

more good news. As Fort Worth entered the 1920s, the mission dedicated its new chapel with the largest crowd to date assembled in the building. On January 18, 1920, seminary president Lee Scarborough preached to more than 750 people about "What Does God Do With Our Sins?" And on the next day, January 19, the remodeling of a large corner room into an attractive, well-equipped reading room would begin.[10]

One financial campaign seemed to follow another. In September, directors announced plans to raise enough money to retire the remaining $29,000 debt on the building, as well as install additional showers and a barbershop. Running concurrently with the campaign would be a sixty-day revival accompanied each night by a twelve-piece orchestra and twenty-five-voice choir.[11]

By the following September, the mission's leaders had achieved most of the campaign objectives. At a formal opening Fort Worth citizens were invited to attend a reception and see for themselves the new shower baths and barbershop, as well as an upper floor that had been transformed into a hotel to accommodate sixty-five working men at a nominal cost.[12]

That same month, Mayfield hosted a banquet for members of the mission board, as well as city and county officials, to celebrate the opening of yet another mission department. Introduced by Dr. H. E. Stout, Mayfield was praised for his many contributions. The *Star-Telegram* reported that this dedicated man "who for years preached daily on the streets of Fort Worth from boxes, water plugs and later from the back seat of an automobile" listened as Stout heaped praises on him before a crowd that included many of the movers and shakers of the city. Dr. Stout said that Mayfield stood out as "the great personality of the mission" and that he had "deviled the life out of us to build this plant to care for the city's unfortunate by bringing the three-fold blessing of 'soup, soap and salvation.'" Ever the fundraiser, Mayfield used

the occasion to urge those present to support the mission. His optimism and encouragement were warranted. With a new chapel on the first floor, rooms for men on the second and third floors, and a basement complete with a hot water system, showers, dressing rooms, and a barbershop, the mission was now especially impressive.[13]

That year, as the Christmas season approached, Sam announced bigger plans than ever. The mission would increase the number of food baskets distributed to Fort Worth's needy to 250. To no one's surprise, another campaign was launched to raise $1,250 for the baskets and also for a Christmas dinner at the mission for newsboys and men away from home. A friend of the mission donated a young heifer to be slaughtered for the dinner. Reverend W. H. Coleman of the First Methodist Episcopal Church South in Mineral Wells came to speak on the topic "Your Part and Mine in Setting the World Right," followed by Baptist evangelist W.H. Knight, who preached on the scripture "Enter ye in by the straight gate into life, for broad is the way and wide is the gate that leads to destruction." Nine conversions followed Brother Knight's sermon, bringing that year's total to 619.[14]

While making Christmas plans for the mission, Sam Mayfield was also looking beyond Fort Worth for the good work that might be done in other places. Pursuing that purpose, he invited Pat B. Withrow of Charleston, West Virginia, to speak. Withrow headed a chain of Gospel missions in the South. On the November afternoon he spoke, the crowd was so large that many were turned away. Addressing the subject "How to Get Rich Quick," Withrow told the crowd that "riches are not measured in money but in service to God" and declared his intention to establish several missions in Texas—perhaps six or eight. If these plans were to materialize, he said, all the new missions would be modeled on the successful ministry of Fort

Worth's Union Gospel Mission.[15]

The year neared a close with a revealing, flattering story in the *Fort Worth Press*. "From insignificant quarters," it reported, "the mission has grown into a magnificent, three-story stone building. . . . The second and third floors are equipped with 65 first class rooms, where shelter is provided for those in need." It described the main floor as containing a large auditorium with a pulpit, where evangelistic services were conducted regularly; in the basement were fourteen shower baths and lavatories. In addition, the article reminded readers that the building and lot originally cost $83,500 and claimed that $12,000 had been spent making improvements. Perhaps most important of all, it reported more than 25,000 conversions at the mission.

The newspaper story could have told even more, for the year had indeed been impressive. More than 36,000 people attended 460 religions services. Thirteen boys and girls taken from the streets had been returned to their homes. Christmas baskets filled with groceries had been delivered to three hundred families and Christmas dinners served to four hundred needy people. Especially striking, the mission had found employment for at least two thousand people.[16]

Sam Mayfield was nothing if not bold and optimistic. He loved to challenge people, as evidenced by the goals he set for 1922. He announced the launching of an evangelical campaign, beginning January 1, that would feature a different speaker every night for more than two months and would aim for two thousand conversions to Jesus Christ. The first preacher was J. W. Bergin of First Methodist Church, followed later in the day by W. W. Rivers of North Side Baptist addressing "What Fort Worth Needs Most in 1922." "It may need a new railroad terminal and post office, as well as new streets and office buildings," he claimed, "but most of all [it] needs God and more religion in

business and everyday life."[17]

Just one week into the campaign, Mayfield was already announcing additional goals. The auditorium had been packed every night, and gifts for the $15,000 annual budget were coming in at such a rate that he expected the campaign to be concluded early in March. When that happened, he was prepared to launch another $20,000 campaign to add two more floors to the mission dormitory, making it a five-story structure. Also, he wanted an additional $15,000 to retire fully the $100,000 cost of the building.[18]

Sam could make a strong case about why the mission not only needed but also deserved support. At a banquet hosted by First Methodist Church, he told ministers, board members, and local government officials that in the span of a little more than three weeks the mission had helped sixty young men paroled from the city jail return to their homes or find work. One of these testified about how he had straightened out his life, thanks to the mission; his testimony was followed by Mayor W. E. Cockrell, who praised the role of Union Gospel Mission in Fort Worth and pledged to clear the streets of those men who could not or would not respond to offers of help. Rev. J. W. Bergin, host pastor, reminded those present that ministers often label people as being either good or bad. "Neither really exists," he claimed. "There is something in a man that will respond to the better impulses, no matter how hardened he may be in his methods of living."[19]

Sam was as busy as ever. While overseeing the campaign, he continued to help the unemployed find work. Realizing that many jobs were out of town, requiring transportation that most men did not have, he committed the mission to pay the railroad fare of those who landed jobs within fifty miles of Fort Worth. Calls for yardmen, gardeners, and repairmen came to the mission from across the area, as did offers from local dairies. In fact, dairies had actually found most of their employees through the mission. Even men arrested on city streets and jailed were helped. In the first five weeks of 1922, thanks to the mission, seventy-two were paroled and placed in jobs. And not just men: employment for a number of women was also found.[20]

Mayfield poured himself into care for the unemployed. In a two-month period he saw that the mission furnished 750 meals to the jobless and sent mission workers throughout Fort Worth and to adjoining towns looking for employment opportunities. He even increased the free railroad fare to a seventy-five mile trip and called on people across the city to donate clothes to men and women who were still out of work.[21]

Sometimes Mayfield had to take special initiative, as in the case of a young man arrested for vagrancy. H. Brinsfield, from Visalia, California, claimed he had been arrested for vagrancy after already obtaining a job. He had arrived in Fort Worth on a Saturday night and was promised a job that was to begin on Tuesday. However, on Monday he had been arrested while going to a room furnished by Sam Mayfield. He was told not to worry, that the police would "give him a bed" at the city jail. His request to call Sam was denied. At his trial he simply told his story, was fined and taken to the county road crew to work it off. When Sam eventually received a letter from him, describing what had happened, he could not believe it. He quickly intervened, obtained Brinsfield's release, and found him a job as a truck driver.[22]

No sooner had this young man been rescued by Sam than another one, also sent to a county road crew for vagrancy, pleaded for help. Working on these road crews was no easy sentence. Prisoners were actually shackled and had to work for hours at a time under grueling conditions. Seventeen-year-old Albert Watkins had come to Fort Worth from Lansing, Michigan, and had been arrested and charged with vagrancy by a Texas and Pacific Railway detective. He pleaded guilty, and like Brinsfield, was fined one dollar plus costs, then put to work on the county road. Shortly before completing his sentence, he developed a blister on his ankle from the shackles and, upon his discharge, went to Union Gospel Mission of Tarrant County for help with employment. The blister soon became infected and so serious that Mayfield had him admitted to a hospital and oversaw his medical care.[23]

The mission was thriving. An audit covering a thirty-three-month period showed that $102,546.54 had been paid on the building debt, leaving an indebtedness of only $13,500. And the $30,000 campaign to add three floors to the building for additional rooms was well underway. Mayfield reported that during the previous three months 108 sermons had been preached, with 6,700 in attendance, 189 converts, and 268 requests for prayer. On the employment front, 266 men had been placed in jobs and 285 beds had been furnished free to those out of work.[24]

Mayfield was not one to be satisfied with the status quo, however. In May, he announced that activities of the mission would be greatly increased during the summer, with the hope of making it headquarters for railroad men in Fort Worth. Accordingly, the mission would reopen the recently completed baths for the summer, install reading rooms with free stationery, and fulfill plans to install a cafeteria. Meals would be 30 percent below average restaurant prices, and baths would cost the railroaders only one dollar per month.[25]

When summer arrived that year, Reverend W. W. Rivers was preaching on "Hell and How to Get There," and the work of the mission was growing so rapidly that Sam Mayfield asked the board of directors for an assistant. Several months earlier, Frank Holzhauser of St. Louis, who had been converted at the mission, had donated an organ for the mission's use. Now Sam hired him as "religious work" secretary and musical director. Holzhauser had become involved with mission work in several cities and was especially proficient at piano, organ, and gospel singing. Now Sam brought him back to Union Gospel Mission of Tarrant County as assistant superintendent, specializing in religious work and music.[26]

Once again the mission made a strong showing in Sam's midsummer report. During the first six months of 1922, the mission had conducted 165 worship services attended by 15,945 people. It had recorded 341 conversions to Jesus Christ, furnished 365 free beds, served 545 free meals, and sent thirty-five telegrams requesting help for young men. Also, jobs had been found for 365 people, and twenty-nine letters were written to boys in prison. The jail ministry had been especially impressive. Seventy-eight worship services were conducted there, and ninety-eight clothing items, plus four pairs of shoes, had been distributed. Perhaps most telling, Sam Mayfield had gotten sixty-five men out of jail and off the county road crews. Revealing that some of the young men being helped by the mission were actually children, the report said that seven boys under the age of fifteen were sent back to their parents after being released by the courts. A local newspaper called this "one of the most satisfactory periods of the history of the institution." In no other period had the mission been able to minister relief to such a large number.[27]

But preaching and conversions remained at the heart of the mission's work, and every so often a widely known speaker appeared. Such was the case in October 1922, when Rev. Bud Robinson, a nationally renowned evangelist, came to preach. Robinson's story was well known. He had been converted at a brush-arbor revival in South Texas in 1877, after hearing a sermon by Rev. James A. Walkup. This signal event in his life was almost accidental. As a wagon carrying his family passed the brush arbor, Bud jumped off to listen to some preaching. So fascinat-ed was he that he went back that night to hear more, then "hired out" to a farmer near there and kept returning during the next days until finally coming forward to accept Jesus Christ.

Robinson preached at the mission on a Tuesday night. So many people came that a large number had to be turned away at the door. Among those assembled were many Fort Worth ministers. Robinson, touting his credentials, told the crowd that he had preached for forty-two years, had averaged four hundred sermons a year, and traveled 700,000 miles.[28]

One never quite knew what kind of message he or she might hear at the mission worship services. While Bud Robinson sought conversions, Methodist Bishop E. L. Waldorf came to describe fools. Before a large crowd, he divided them into five categories: fair-weather fools, fools who do not count the cost, fools with no insight or foresight, no-God fools, and fools who live only for this world. "The man with a defective head, a bad heart and a string for backbone is the worst type of fool," he said. "Men are made fools by bad women, by living to dress rather than dressing to live . . . by money, by failure to take the right direction from friends, or he may be a natural-born fool." Few were spared.[29]

As Christmas approached that year, mission workers again began preparing baskets of food for the needy. Sam had surveyed the city's needs to see what might be most helpful. Each basket contained enough food to last several days, including meat, a sack of flour, sugar, coffee and bread. Just before Christmas, a group of men and women spent an entire day distributing the baskets and clothing. In addition, Sam was planning a Christmas Day dinner for three hundred homeless boys and men.[30]

The dinner was strikingly successful. Several hundred men, women, and children attended, including "the lame, the blind, and the stranger within the gates." Rev. J. W. Bergin of First Methodist Church preached. Then all were treated to a Christmas turkey dinner, and toys were distributed to the children. All this was followed by singing, which stretched the celebration to almost three hours.[31]

It had been a good year. Hundreds of those in need had been fed and clothed, given beds, jobs, transportation, and encouragement to improve their lives. In 1922 alone, almost forty thousand people had attended some 475 services under the auspices of Union Gospel Mission of Tarrant County, held everywhere from railroad shops and factories to jails and open-air meetings.[32]

Throughout this period the mission's ties to the railroad remained strong. In the spring of 1923 Sam Mayfield announced that the seventh annual meeting of Texas railroad men would soon be held there. Partitions were removed from the auditorium in order to double its capacity—and with good reason. In June, several hundred railroad-related people arrived to hear music that included First Methodist Church's orchestra and preaching by Ollie Webb of the Texas and Pacific Railway. Webb reminded the crowd that evangelist Bud Robinson would soon be returning and urged them "to get up spiritual steam in advance of his coming" in order to make the most of the occasion. He preached that day on Jesus's parable of the talents, saying: "It isn't what a man has that he will have to answer to God for, but what he has done with what he was given." Sam Mayfield had set a goal of a thousand conversions in two weeks. One of three men who came forward following Webb's sermon brought the year's total to 410. Mayfield expected to reach the goal with the help of Bud Robinson.[33]

Toward the end of June, as promised, Bud Robinson returned to Union Gospel Mission of Tarrant County, again drawing overflow crowds. On a Sunday afternoon he preached on the subject for which he was best known: "The Two Works of Grace." Robinson contended that there is a difference between what a man is by nature and by actual transgression. He believed in what he called the "two works of grace." That is, justification or forgiveness of sin is what God does for us; sanctification is what God works in us. Robinson laid out his beliefs the way he had done so many times before. No longer a Methodist, he was now a member of the Church of the Nazarene, claiming that it came closest to proclaiming the old-time Methodist doctrine.[34] At this appearance Robinson attacked the theory of evolution and those who supported it. But he saved his heaviest salvos for the tobacco industry, calling smoking one of the largest contributors to the creation of criminals. As evidence, he told of preaching in a prison where 490 of 525 inmates questioned had smoked from their youth. This, he contended, was a major contributor to their errant ways.[35]

Bud Robinson was followed the next evening by Rev. E. W. Wells, who shared the story of his life and how being converted to Jesus Christ at a Cleburne revival twelve years earlier had saved him from a life of gambling and drinking. He told his hearers that, following his very first sermon, five bootleggers came forward, three of whom were saved. At the close of the service, Wells announced the subject of his next day's sermon: "Hell With Fire in It."[36]

By that summer Sam was declaring the mission to be in its best financial condition ever. The entire plant was valued at $165,000, and outstanding debt was only $7,500. Moreover, plans had already been drawn to add two more stories to the building, which would make another 150 beds available.[37]

At the same time, through the mission's employment bureau, he was trying to help cotton farmers find cotton pickers. In Alvarado alone, about one hundred were needed. The president of the chamber of commerce had written him seeking help, saying that conditions were favorable for a bountiful season. Sam supplied as many men as possible. Then, true to form, before leaving on vacation, he announced that, upon his return, he would launch a campaign to retire the $7,500 debt and raise another $35,000 to build the two additional floors he wanted.[38]

During these years the mission was part of a growing movement. In May 1925, Mayfield, attending the Association of Gospel Rescue Missions in Washington, DC, announced that additional Texas missions were planned for Dallas, Houston, and probably San Antonio. Two years later the executive committee of the International Union of Gospel Missions was meeting in Fort Worth to announce a nationwide expansion program. Ten new missions had been founded in the preceding twelve months, and one was being projected for every major American city. Supporting this welcome news, Sam announced that Fort Worth would be bidding to host the 1928 national convention.[39]

By this time, Union Gospel Mission of Tarrant County had done some major expanding of its own. In the summer of 1925, Sam Mayfield made one of the biggest announcements in the mission's history. A $100,000 contract had been let for the construction of a new, second mission building. Southwell & Abbott contractors would build it at the corner of Houston and Fifteenth Streets. John Lancaster, the Texas and Pacific Railway president, had encouraged the project, which would serve railroad men and give them a place to stay between shifts. The building, with four stories plus a basement, was estimated to cost $150,000 and would raise the mission's total property value to $300,000.[40]

During the next months, as the building went up, the mission continued to host an array of local preachers and oversee an amazing range of programs. The 1925 annual report was especially revealing. While posting numbers, it reflected, as one of its categories so colorfully described, the "backsliders reclaimed," the gospel preached, the hungry fed, and lives turned around.

These numbers told the story of just this one year:

Religious services conducted at the mission, railroad shops, factories, open air, and jail ............................ 382

Total attendance at all services ................. 29,653

Conversions .................................................. 360

Requests for prayer ..................................... 978

Backsliders reclaimed .................................. 109

Visits to the sick ........................................... 91

Bibles and Testaments distributed ................... 101

Shoes distributed – pairs .............................. 96

Garments distributed .................................... 187

Letters written to boys and their mothers ................................................ 58

Christmas baskets filled sent to families ........ 305

Christmas dinners given to the poor .............. 298

Total number of poor helped Christmas ....... 1,926

Free beds given during the year ...................... 819

Free meals given during the year ................. 1,021

Employment found for .............................. 1,938

Seeking employment at the mission............ 8,500

Groceries and meat donated....................... $900

(Signed) S. B. Mayfield, Superintendent.

Financially the mission was also in good shape, having raised $31,400.56 that year and finishing 1925 with money in the bank.[41]

As optimism spilled over into 1926, one of the most dramatic events imaginable happened. On February 4, as the new building neared completion, L. B. Price of Greenwich, Connecticut, spoke at the annual banquet of mission directors. A wealthy businessman, Price was a director of the Federated Boys Clubs. He had come to Fort Worth to help Union Gospel Mission of Tarrant County found a local Boys Club, a cause he fervently supported.

In his speech to some of the city's wealthiest men, he quoted the Bible and told them it was their duty to use their gains for philanthropic purposes. "Someday," he said, "I will stand before the final judgment. I will be asked if I prospered in business while on earth. My answer will be 'yes.' Then I will be asked if I helped the under dogs on earth. I tell you gentlemen, I would be afraid not to devote my time and money to this work." He concluded by saying, "There is more value in saving one boy from going to the devil than there is in all the money in Fort Worth." He announced a campaign for a Boys Club by pledging $1,000.00.

Then came the unexpected. No sooner had Price sat down than he turned ashen, collapsed, and fell to the floor. Attendants rushed to help him but discovered there was nothing to be done. He was dead. The stunned audience of more than two hundred watched helplessly as efforts to resuscitate Price failed, and he was transported to Harris Sanitarium. Sam Mayfield, in a rare understatement, said: "That was the most dramatic thing I have ever heard." The *Star-Telegram* reported that, following Price's death, "the meeting of the mission directors was adjourned."[42]

Two months later, the mission's new building opened. Sam invited more than two hundred prominent businessmen and women to a formal dedication ceremony. Devoted to railroad men, the building had one hundred modern, windowed rooms on the second, third and fourth floors, with baths on each floor. It was valued at $160,000 and advertised as a place "where men are helped to help themselves." By July, thanks largely to the Railroad Men's Hotel, the outreach of the mission had almost doubled. And by October of the following year, when the International Union of Gospel Missions met in Fort Worth to plan the expansion of its work, Fort Worth's mission was hailed as the second largest mission in the nation.[43]

By October 1926, another campaign was underway to finance the coming year. Board member W. B. Fishburn, campaign chair, spelled out powerfully what was at stake. Since its founding, he claimed, "Union Gospel Mission on lower Main Street has been the stage for one of life's greatest dramas—the struggle of man for existence and, after that, for eternal life." The campaign goal was $25,000, which would fund many of the ministries being undertaken by the mission at that time: evangelical work, jail services and welfare, employment for young and old, visits to the sick, distribution of Bibles, food and fuel for the needy, meals and beds for desperate men, and a home for transient railway men. The purpose of all this, said Fishburn, was "to get a person's heart and life right so that he will make good." He pointed to the mission's record of 29,000 conversions to Christianity—"hundreds of human driftwood salvaged for society, of convicts turned to a life of rectitude and usefulness" as proof of the mission's value.[44]

Fishburn bolstered his campaign case with the assertion that the mission, rather than competing with local churches, was providing a service that the church could not provide. "It reaches the man and woman of the street," he claimed, "all classes of them. At services I have seen the man in overalls bowed down by the side of the man of wealth. I have seen at our services men who have not been in church for 10 years. The mission is the outpost of every church in the city."[45]

Fishburn had good reason to boast. During the previous year, many men, women, and children had been helped in various ways by the mission. Groceries and fuel had been given to three thousand people. Free meals were provided for 1,310 "homeless and friendless men and boys," free beds to 832 destitute men and boys. In addition, the mission had found work for 8,500 people and recorded 567 conversions and "blacksliders reclaimed." It had also distributed 2,525 Bibles and conducted 292 services in the county jail.[46]

The mission was not restricted to grown men. Boys were there, too. Left adrift by broken families, a number of boys wound up at the mission, where they could live for $1.50 a week until they became entirely self-sufficient. The demand was such that as soon as one boy left, another quickly stepped into his place.[47]

When a needy person appeared at the mission door, several things happened right away. He was first given food and then a place to bathe and sleep. Next he was sent to the mission's employment bureau where he was matched with a job. At this stage of the mission's life, residents were invited but not required to attend worship services held nightly, as well as every Sunday afternoon.[48]

Jail services were also a well-known, important aspect of the mission's work. Every Sunday morning a volunteer known as "Mother" Teel and other workers went to every ward of the jail to pray, read the Bible, and visit with the prisoners. Sam Mayfield especially valued this ministry and claimed that conversions were numerous. He was particularly concerned about young people who wound up in jail and told of four young men between the ages of eighteen and twenty who were placed in the Tarrant County jail while on their way from El Paso to the Huntsville penitentiary. Mayfield got to know them and corresponded with them throughout their prison terms. Upon release, three of the young men returned to Fort Worth, found jobs through Union Gospel Mission of Tarrant County, and led productive lives.[49]

As the decade of the 1920s neared an end, mission president T. B. Hoffer claimed, "There is nothing sensational in this work. It is unostentatious in its methods. Nevertheless there are literally hundreds whose lives have been changed and uplifted through the Gospel faithfully presented by Mr. Mayfield . . . and the fine ministers of this city. . . . Success has been ours." In the summer of 1929, Mayfield, while taking no personal credit, called the previous year "the greatest year in our history"—the greatest evangelistic services, the greatest number of conversions, the "greatest number

of homeless, jobless, friendless and penniless men and boys given free beds and meals," as well as the greatest number of prisoners who heard the Gospel in the Tarrant County jail. "We are you and your church at work," he continued, "taking God's message and ministry of love to the prisons, hospitals, almshouses, shut-ins and the slums."[50]

The mission's report for 1928 was both impressive and instructive. More than 1,400 free beds for "men and boys out of work" were provided, 1,112 free meals served, 1,527 jobs furnished, more than three thousand men from thirty-two counties assisted, and 27,800 people had attended worship services that year. In addition, receipts for the year were $47,528.05. When a January 1, 1928, balance of $3,024.48 was included, total receipts reached $50,552.53. Disbursements that year were $43,754.36, leaving a December 31, 1928, balance of $6,798.17. The report also profiled several men who, once helped by the mission, were now leading successful lives. For instance, Clinton Huddleston of Denver, Colorado, who was converted at the mission in 1916, had become a deacon in a Baptist church and preached often at a local mission. A. F. Puckett of Fort Worth, converted at the mission in 1921, had become not only a Baptist church deacon but also a city policeman and a "God-fearing, home-loving" man. Richard Miller, who had been converted at the mission in 1914 and become a successful cement contractor in Chicago, was especially praised because he had been "greatly under the influence of whiskey when converted," and the "Good Lord delivered him from the awful curse of the old rum demon."[51]

In the summer of 1929, the mission board of directors included new members Mark McMahon, Grover Cole, S. D. Johnson, John B. Collier Jr., and C. Pendleton, all added that year. Directors reelected were T. B. Hoffer, W. D. Smith, Max Bergman, L. A. McWhirter, Dr. Paul Lipps, J. R. Penn, E. E. Plaxco, Dr. L. R. Scarborough, J. R. Edwards, W. E. Allen, W. Yates, W. N. Hinckley, G. C. Poston, W. B. LaCava, A. C. Barber, John G. Farmer, O. W. Williams, C. S. Elliot, Ben T. Scott, W. M. Green, and from St. Louis, D. Van Gieson. The advisory committee reelected W. E. Connell, chairman; A. J. Duncan, Willard Burton, William Monnig, A. E. Thomas, and A. F. Townsend. Sam Mayfield was reelected superintendent.[52]

Despite their impressive successes, Fort Worth and Union Gospel Mission of Tarrant County were not isolated from national events.

In October 1929 the stock market crashed, creating what would soon become the Great Depression. Unemployment held steady for a few months but then exploded, putting people out of their homes, onto the streets, and into soup lines. The situation became so bad that some people even scavenged for food in the trash bins at restaurant and hotel back doors. Conditions quickly created not only an economic disaster but, for many people, a personal one as well.[53]

# CHAPTER FOUR

For a while Fort Worth escaped the Great Depression's full impact, due primarily to a building boom that had already been set in motion. Late in the 1920s Fort Worth citizens had passed $100 million in bond issues for construction of roads, bridges, and buildings for public use. A state improvement program had furnished another $50 million for these projects. One local conventioneer at a Fort Worth business-related meeting rebuffed the notion that there was anything "depressing in the business outlook out where the West begins," and the general manager of the National Association of Insurance Writers said, "Texans don't know what a depression is. They ought to be in the East."[1]

However, Fort Worth citizens were soon to learn what a depression was. Transients began arriving in town hoping for construction jobs but discovering that they were already filled. Work was about to begin on dams for Eagle Mountain and Bridgeport lakes, but every job was taken. A headline declared "1,000 Unemployed Invade City to Seek Work on Two Dams," and an editorial declared that the city was "fast becoming a Mecca for 'floating' laborers (and) drifters." At Union Gospel Mission, the 165 unemployed men who sat for supper on an evening early in 1930 came from thirty-one states. Soon men were raking leaves in a downtown park as part of a makeshift work program, and conditions were so critical by 1932 that the city appropriated one hundred dollars a month to operate a soup kitchen.[2]

Emblematic of the desperation was a Fort Worth family who, upon being evicted from their home, parked a covered wagon downtown beside the Trinity River and set up camp. Next to them was a family of eight, all living in one old car. The city responded by creating a tourist camp for these and other people in similar straits and by trying to find extra beds in the City-County Hospital. But the hospital was overwhelmed with 7,510 flu cases in 1931. That number would explode to 36,433 the next year. The situation deteriorated to the point that, for the first time, officials at city hall actually locked the hospital doors "to prevent its passageways from being converted into a dormitory by the disinherited 'floaters.'"

Religious groups, as well as individuals, tried to help. For instance, a church in Keller, after hearing that drifters at Union Gospel Mission of Tarrant County had little to eat, donated a live steer. One of the volunteers knew someone at the Bluebonnet Packing Company who dressed and prepared the steer free of charge.

Despite the hard times, mission leaders pressed ahead, making plans and sharing hopes. In January 1930, W. D. Smith was elected president of the board of directors, succeeding T. B. Hoffer. That same month Sam Mayfield announced that the International Convention of Union Gospel Missions would be coming to town in May, bringing leading officials of missions around the nation and Canada, as well as delegates who would be filling local pulpits on the Sunday of the meeting. As superintendent of Union Gospel Mission of Tarrant County, he would act as host to the delegates.[3]

When the convention opened early in May at the Hotel Texas, more than two hundred delegates and their wives were in attendance. It quickly became a whirlwind of activity, cheerleading, and goal setting. On Sunday morning, mission directors from across the country preached in local congregations. That same afternoon and evening they held large meetings to discuss the direction of their organization and to hear inspirational messages. Ted Becker, president of the association, predicted that one day a chain of Union Gospel Missions would extend around the globe into every country. Field Secretary J. A. Schlichter followed Becker and reported that many missions were struggling because of the Depression, but were needed more than ever. His own story supported his case. "For fifteen years I used more than forty grams of morphine a day and drank excessively," he said. "My father was a minister and died of a broken heart while I was tramping about the country under an assumed name." Just one drink "given to me by a banker's daughter and the assurance that it would not harm me to be a 'moderate drinker' started me on the road to the depths. I am one of the fortunate few who ever 'came back' after taking to morphine." He credited Jesus Christ with saving his life. "We cannot be worth much to others until we are worth something to ourselves, and we will not be worth much to ourselves until we are worth something to our Lord." He, too, called for a mission in every city around the world that could support one.[4]

Near the close of the convention, one of the association's officers, E. R. McKinney, took aim at what he considered the worst evils of the day. Movies headed his list. "Millions of American citizens are daily gazing upon lewd, lustful motion pictures designed to obliterate every high ideal in the nation," he declared. They "are destroying our purity of morals and

desecrating the Sabbath." Next were colleges. "Professors in many of our schools are atheists and are aiding the movement to defeat Christianity." Tobacco manufacturers were no better. Their advertisements, "showing pictures of young girls smoking is another finger pointing toward the unrighteousness of this age." Crime, too, was singled out as being "more rampant in this country than any other in the world. It is the beginning of a communism and Bolshevism that has wrecked other countries." When the meeting finally closed, Sam Mayfield declared it "one of the outstanding conventions in the history of the missions."[5]

Union Gospel Mission of Tarrant County, although dealing with the neediest of the needy and the temporarily down and out, was clearly seen as an integral, even honored, part of Fort Worth's life. A telling example occurred in November 1931, when the new twelve-story Texas and Pacific passenger station was dedicated. John L. Lancaster, president of the railroad, was feted for bringing this magnificent facility to Fort Worth; it capped off a $13 million railroad-building program in the city. The day included a long parade, the formal presentation of the station, and speeches by Amon G. Carter and W. A. Hanger. The festivities culminated in a large luncheon honoring John L. Lancaster at Union Gospel Mission of Tarrant County. The mission's strong ties to the railroad, as well as its prominent place in the city's affairs, made this the obvious thing to do.

A few months later, the mission became involved in a project no one had planned—helping a local orphanage survive and expand. In Fort Worth, following the stock market crash in 1929, Lena Pope had begun caring for abandoned, homeless children. As their numbers swelled, she desperately needed more space. By 1932, even after moving to larger quarters, she was again out of room. Because the county had placed several children in her home, this time she approached the county for help, requesting two rock dormitories to be built behind the main house. If the county would agree to haul stone to the site, she would find a way to build the dormitories.[6]

One day, while searching for stone seventeen miles from town, Lena Pope spotted, at the front gate of a ranch, a woman chasing turkeys near a pile of stone. After helping the woman catch the turkeys, Pope inquired about the stone and was told she could have all she wanted. Union Gospel Mission of Tarrant County was soon involved. Sam Mayfield, made aware of this situation, sent men out to break and load the stone onto trucks. Others joined the cause. The Fort Worth School Board supplied lunches for the workers from school leftovers, while merchant Marvin Leonard donated picks and shovels. Lena Pope recruited two stone masons. Boys from the orphanage dug the foundation, and a contractor, seeing what needed to be done, volunteered to build the dormitories. And so it happened, thanks in no small part to Sam Mayfield's initiative and leadership.[7]

As Fort Worth struggled to survive the Depression, the mission continued to care for the needy and to maintain, as much as possible, its traditional schedule of events. The annual banquet was one such occasion. In October 1934, John Lancaster, president of the Texas and Pacific Railway, was the special guest and featured speaker. Attended by two hundred of the city's leading business and professional men, the banquet was held on the main floor of the new Texas and Pacific Railway Station. The rest of the building was empty—intentionally. Lancaster said that he would wait until the Depression ended to rent out the upper floors, so as not to empty other Fort Worth buildings in hard times.

That evening Lancaster tried to find good in the midst of difficult days. He reminded mission board members and other guests that hard times had turned people's attention away from money toward aspects of life more worthwhile, such as city beautification, family life, friend-

ship with neighbors, and sympathy for the less fortunate. He was especially impressed with Fort Worth's beautification projects, in particular the creation of Rock Springs Park. "I have never seen a more lovely park," he said. "That it was built against obstacles you may be sure, but give me the man any time who can achieve much with little means as against the man who has millions to work with." And as he often did, Lancaster praised Mayfield and his wife for all they had accomplished at the mission.[8]

In January 1935, at a meeting held again in the Texas and Pacific Railway passenger station, nine new members joined the board of directors: L. C. Porter, C. T. Wilhoit, Pete A. Pickel, G. J. Bennett, Albert McCleland, Roy Miller, J. A. Tadlock, Earl Mitchell, and Roy B. Curby. They were chosen by a nominating committee composed of W. D. Smith, chairman; T. H. Wilhelm, John Thompson, R. L. Truitt, and J. G. Whittmayer. The next month Galen J. Bennett was elected president of the board of directors.[9]

As the Great Depression continued and the ranks of the unemployed swelled, demands on Union Gospel Mission of Tarrant County grew heavier. At an April 1935 dinner, the mission's care for "the least of these" was lavishly praised by local pastors. "Our churches go as far as they can," said Rev. W. R. White of Broadway Baptist Church, "but there still remains that outer fringe that the churches cannot touch. Those persons . . . would be ineffectively touched by Christianity, if touched at all, were it not for Union Gospel Mission." Episcopal minister E. H. Ecke called the mission "the friend of the floater, the down-and-outer, the hobo." And Rev. W. H. Cole, urging churches to support the mission, said: "As long as the story of the Good Samaritan is read, the church must do more than simply make a gesture toward those who have fallen by the roadside."[10]

Sam Mayfield bolstered the case by announcing some impressive numbers. During the previous twelve months 372 evangelistic services had been attended by 22,120 people. Moreover, there had been 1,004 conversions, 1,450 people ministered to at the altar, and 675 "backsliders reclaimed." And three months later he was able to announce that during the first six months of 1935, collections on subscriptions (pledges) to the mission were 25 percent ahead of the same time period in 1934.[11]

As if times were not trying enough, on the last day of September 1935, a two-alarm fire broke out in the mission's railroad building. Thirty-four men, wearing their nightshirts, scrambled out of beds into the street. While building damage was not severe, the fire gutted a nearby café. No men were killed, but the same could not be said of eight canaries and a pet sparrow.[12] Several new directors were elected in January 1936: N. E. Buster, L. E. Davis, S. F. Dugger, Knox Faires, J. W. Grimes, C. W. Leftwich, Jack McGraw, Earl Mitchell, and Robert Welborn.[13] The advent of the new year did not lighten the mission's load. In fact, January and February became the busiest months in its history. In that period alone, 147 families were helped and 1,158 individuals received food, clothing, fuel, lodging, bedding, and aid of one sort or another. In addition, 575 clothing items, including hundreds of pairs of shoes and forty pieces of bedding, were distributed. In those two months, a record number of meals were served, fifty-seven worship services were conducted, and sixty-one conversions recorded.[14]

By that fall, the mission was experiencing major challenges. State relief funds remained low, and the federal government was cutting much of its emergency aid. As winter persisted, hard times continued, and the mission's workload was especially heavy. Preparing for a year-end board meeting at the Westbrook Hotel, M. J. Thomas, chairman of the mission's relief committee, said, "Last year it was necessary to administer practical aid to 12,786 persons. Undoubtedly, the number will show an increase this year if the mission meets the demands of the poor. For forty-eight years," he continued, "this organization has conducted charity work, and its greatest year in service rendered was the one just closing." Sympathy for the less fortunate, as John Lancaster had predicted a few years before, was strong. In fact, 96 percent of 1936 pledges had been collected by year's end.[15] In January 1937, board officers and members were as follows: G. J. Bennett, president; L. C. Porter, vice president; C. S. Elliot, recording secretary; E. E. Flippo, treasurer; and George R. Angell, chairman of finances. Directors were M. J. Thomas, A. B. Waldron, E. E. Taylor, W. D. Smith, John A. Thompson, J. M. Sprekelmeyer, J. A. Tadlock, N. E. Buster, Robert T. Welborn, Earl Mitchell, R. F. Duggan, Jack McGraw, and O. E. Crossey.[16]

The mission pushed its way through 1937. That fall, as its leaders planned another annual banquet, they were not yet through honoring John Lancaster. On a Monday night in September, Sam Mayfield was praised for leading the "downtown church in overalls" which, with a $12,000 budget, was giving both material and spiritual aid to hundreds of destitute citizens. Then it was Lancaster's turn. "It is true as rumored," he declared, "that all the happiness we can ever know in this life is what we do for the happiness of others. It's not given to us to enjoy anything by ourselves, and Sam Mayfield's cause for the down and outers . . . is worthy of your support and mine."[17]

During the next weeks, as 1937 waned, so did Sam Mayfield's health. On January 12 of the new year, he was admitted to Methodist Hospital. He underwent surgery and remained in critical condition for several days before he died at 1:30 a.m. on January 16, 1938. He was sixty-eight years old.[18]

For nearly thirty years Sam Mayfield had headed Union Gospel Mission of Tarrant County. He and the mission were almost inseparable. He had literally given his life to its work. His energy, his strong Christian faith, his creativity and optimism, his remarkable ability to relate to those wandering the streets as well as to Fort Worth's leaders—all rolled into one man—were the mission's driving force, in fact its very identity, for nearly three decades. His inspiring qualities, plus his ability to raise money for a wide range of mission programs—to keep campaign after campaign going—not only ensured the survival of Union Gospel Mission of Tarrant County, but also kept its name and good works in the public eye. Sam's exuberance, optimism, and commitment to the cause, his knack for publicizing and promoting, kept the mission in the news and gave it a recognizable face—his. People would have a hard time thinking of Union Gospel Mission of Tarrant County without, at the same time, picturing Sam Mayfield.[19]

# CHAPTER FIVE

The mission did not have time to mourn Sam's passing for long. It needed to move ahead, and Sam was soon followed as superintendent by another remarkable man: Joseph Franklin Green. Green was born on February 12, 1890, in McMinnville, Tennessee, the seventh of twelve children. He had a hard vagabond childhood, working at age eight or nine in a cotton mill before running away from home in the fifth grade. He traveled the country for several years. While visiting an older brother in North Texas, he was converted at a Baptist revival meeting. He eventually came under the influence of a minister named Bowers who encouraged him to finish his education. Green entered a private Baptist school and, at age twenty-four, earned his high school diploma. From there he went to Union University in Jackson, Tennessee, where he met Nell Vesta Kilby and married her in 1923. Next was Baylor University in Waco, where he graduated in 1925, and then Southwestern Baptist Theological Seminary. After graduating in 1938, he accepted the invitation to become superintendent of Union Gospel Mission of Tarrant County.[1]

Although relatively short in stature, Joseph Green had a sturdy build, a large voice, and commanding presence. Premature gray hair gave him a dignified presence. He appeared always to be in control of his surroundings.[2]

No sooner had Green become superintendent than it was time for another annual fund drive. In October 1938, members of the board of directors, under the leadership of President G. J. Bennett, met at the Westbrook Hotel to plan the drive, distribute campaign supplies, and receive their marching orders. The fundraising rested primarily on them. Green had already begun cutting expenses, and the board adopted a budget goal of $11,200, a lower target than the previous year.[3]

When Green became superintendent, the mission was operating out of its two primary buildings. The gray stone main building at Fourteenth and Main Streets, containing offices, a chapel, and sleeping space for homeless men, hosted nightly services. Most of these featured hellfire and brimstone sermons, calling listeners to repentance and conversion. Each service was followed by a meal, often a stew of potatoes, carrots, onions, and beef. Purchasing large quantities of beef allowed the mission to get cut-rate prices at a local packinghouse. With the Depression still taking its toll, more than one hundred men were served nightly. On Sundays, because of evening worship services in many churches, mission services were held in the afternoon, followed by an early supper. The other facility, at Fifteenth and Houston, continued to serve railroad men primarily, and did so successfully.[4]

By the fall of 1939, Green was able to announce that during the coming winter he expected to be serving an average of three thousand hot meals each month in the mission's warm dining room. In the summer, when men could more easily work outdoors for food, he anticipated serving 1,200 breakfasts and dinners

J. L. Lancaster (left) of Dallas, is honored as a best friend of Union Gospel Mission of Tarrant County, October of 1940. J. F. Green, the mission superintendent, stands at center; at right is W.D. Smith. *Courtesy Fort Worth Star-Telegram* collection, Special Collections, the University of Texas at Arlington Library, Arlington, Texas.

monthly. At that time the mission could house and provide beds for eighty men.[5]

Evenings at the mission followed a simple routine. Supper, which usually consisted of stew or vegetables, beef, and cheese, was followed by a 7:30 to 8:30 worship service in the chapel. On Friday, Saturday, and Sunday nights, students from the Southwestern Baptist Theological Seminary preached and led the services. A local pastor took charge on Thursdays, and Joseph Green preached on the other three nights of the week.[6]

Though its work was progressing well and its services were reaching increasing numbers of needy people, by 1941 the mission was facing a financial crisis. In 1927, in order to construct the railroad building, the mission had issued

$125,000 worth of bonds to secure a bank note. It defaulted on the bonds, so in June 1941, the Continental National Bank, on behalf of the bondholders, filed suit in the Forty-eighth District Court to foreclose a mortgage and deed of trust on both of the mission's properties. The petition claimed that the mission had defaulted in the amount of $100,000. The bank asked that the properties be sold to satisfy the debt.[7] W.D. Smith, attorney for the bank, who was also acting in behalf of the mission, claimed that the suit was "friendly" and that the mission would not be closed. The legal proceedings continued, however, and in September the court rendered a judgment in favor of the bank and bondholders. It ruled that the mission had defaulted on the bonds and that both principal and interest were owed to bondholders. If the money was not paid, the property—collateral for the bonds—would be sold to satisfy the debt.[8]

Early in November 1941, at a sheriff's sale on the courthouse steps, under orders of the Forty-eighth District Court, the mission's two downtown properties were sold. This apparently dismaying turn of events turned out to be a win-win situation. The buyer was G. J. Bennett, principal bondholder and president of Union Gospel Mission of Tarrant County's board of directors. The price: $25,000. The advantages were obvious for Bennett. He bought a building for $25,000 that was worth $125,000 in 1927. As a bondholder, some of the sale proceeds were due him, so he did not even have to pay the full $25,000. In addition, with the other bondholders now out of the picture, he could do what he pleased with the buildings. The big upside for the mission was that one of its most ardent supporters was now the landlord and could be expected to act in its best interest.[9]

Just as World War I began in Europe and eventually involved the United States, so what would become World War II was about to engulf the country. In December 1941, soon after Pearl Harbor, America mobilized for war. These de-

**At worship in the chapel, 1962.** Courtesy *Fort Worth Star-Telegram* collection, Special Collections, the University of Texas at Arlington Library, Arlington, Texas.

velopments would impact not only Fort Worth as a whole but also Union Gospel Mission of Tarrant County. In August 1942, the mission's property holdings were reduced to one—the hotel building at Houston and Fifteenth. The old building at Fourteenth and Main was sold to Frank M. Anderson, president of Cascade Laundry. Anderson said the purchase was what he termed a "private investment" and that the building would be rented.[10]

The entire operation of the mission was then moved to the hotel building. Necessary adjustments were soon made. The Greens, with their three children, set up housekeeping on the second floor. Each child had a room. Some walls were knocked out to create a kitchen and din-

ing room. The family members shared a single bathroom containing several shower stalls and toilets. The large dining room downstairs was used for worship services, and cots were set up in the basement for the homeless. There was no air conditioning, of course. Large fans pushed the air around.[11]

The evening services were simple, with prayers, scripture readings, and hymns. Only on Sundays was a pianist available, unless a guest pastor brought one along during the week. The men were invited to call out the names of the hymns they wanted to sing. "The Old Rugged Cross," "Are You Washed in the Blood?," "Just As I Am," and "Wonderful Words of Life" were frequent choices. Then, following

Rev. and Mrs. Joseph F. Green prepare a meal at the mission on Houston Street, 1951. *Courtesy Fort Worth Star-Telegram* collection, Special Collections, the University of Texas at Arlington Library, Arlington, Texas.

strong hellfire and brimstone sermons, the men were invited to come forward where they were "counseled and prayed with" before being allowed to line up for supper and receive a bed assignment.[12]

Green looked for promise and possibilities in these men. Those who seemed sincere in their determination to better themselves were offered help finding jobs and also allowed to stay at the hotel. Many found work as painters and carpenters. They began their days with coffee and day-old bread and sweet rolls contributed by local bakeries before heading to jobs they had landed.[13]

These homeless loners who had hit bottom in their lives, literally down and out, were often seen as having no problems more serious than laziness. But in fact many of them were suffering from alcoholism and various degrees of mental illness. There was a growing awareness of alcoholism in society as a whole, but not a widespread interest in understanding it or dealing with it as a disease. Alcoholics were simply drunks who had not gotten their lives together, so there was little motivation to do much about it. The same could be said of mental illness. Few treatment options were available, and alarmingly little was known about many of its forms. The mentally ill were often hidden from view or pushed to the outer fringes of normal, day-to-day life. Many wound up on the streets, neglected and confused. Some found their way to Union Gospel Mission of Tarrant County.[14]

Joseph Green dealt with these troubled people almost single-handedly. With few alcohol treatment programs available and scant resources to help the mentally ill, there was little he could do to address anything larger than the most immediate problems. Awareness of the magnitude of problems presented by alcoholism and mental illness, as well as widespread community-based treatment programs, were still in the future. Green did the best he could, hoping that a welcoming environment, compassion, and the power of God to renew life through the preaching of the Gospel would set these men on a better track.[15]

The work of the mission became a Green family affair. Green's wife, Nell, cooked not only for her own family but also for more than one hundred homeless men who arrived nightly. She was also her husband's secretary and the mission's bookkeeper. Green's ten-year-old son, Leslie, had the daily job of riding his bicycle across Lancaster Street to the post office and picking up the mail. One afternoon in 1942, his mail run turned into an unforgettable experience. While crossing the street, he noticed an olive-colored Cadillac, with stars on the license plate, pulling out into the street from the train station. "I thought it was unusual to be painted that color," he recalled. Sure that he was going to get to see a general, Leslie followed the car, pedaling fast. He was about to give up when the car stopped at the light at Jennings Street. He pedaled up beside a rear window, pressed his face to the glass and, to his astonishment, found himself eye-to-eye with President Franklin Delano Roosevelt. "There was FDR," said Leslie. "He had this amazed look on his face, said 'Hit the gas,' and the car took off."[16]

Leslie hurried back to tell his parents that he had just seen, up close, the president of the United States. His father, sure that it was just a boy's imagination, assured him that he was mistaken and had seen someone who resembled President Roosevelt. "But Dad," he insisted, "I know what the president looks like, and that was him." Leslie begged his father to call John Oster, mission treasurer and Texas and Pacific stationmaster. Green gave in and made the phone call, only to discover to his surprise that, yes, the president was in town. "No one is supposed to know that. How did you find out?" asked Oster. When Green relayed Leslie's adventure, Oster revealed that Roosevelt made regular trips to visit his son, Elliott, who was living in Fort Worth, and that a special platform had been built at the T&P station to take him from the train. "Do not tell anybody," he repeated. "Tell Leslie to keep it quiet."[17]

Although the Green family had moved to the hotel building and become settled, their stay was not to last long. In November 1943, the government announced that transient Air Force officers who had business with the Air Training Command headquarters would occupy the mission's hotel building. The building had recently been leased to the army and would require extensive remodeling to fulfill its new purpose. In order to provide mess facilities for officers, enlisted men, and civilians on duty, for example, a cafeteria would be installed in the basement and a dining mess hall on the first floor. In addition, bachelor quarters for officers permanently stationed there were in the plans, as was an officers' club, which would require that the family living quarters be gutted. Green was not pleased. He hated alcohol. The very thought of an officers' club being right in the middle of what had been his home was repugnant to him.[18]

These developments necessitated two moves. One was the relocation of the mission. Green moved it into a rented store on Houston Street, two blocks north of the mission building. The new quarters were large enough for worship services but not for overnight accommodations. And, of course, Green had to find another home. In the Poly area, at Avenue I and Brinkley—near Texas Wesleyan University—he bought and remodeled a home in which he and his family would live throughout the rest of the war.[19]

When the war ended in 1945, the Green family and the mission moved back into the hotel building, and the operation of the mission became increasingly a family project. Green preached regularly, delivering hell and damnation sermons night after night. Nell Green became associate superintendent, continuing, among other chores, to cook all the meals and keep the books. And by this time Leslie was operating the elevator and working evenings and weekends at the front desk. By the late 1940s, while a freshman at Texas Christian University, he was also preaching two or three times a month.[20]

Joseph Green's December 1947 annual report indicated that the mission was back in full swing. It had served free meals to 7,493 homeless men and given free lodging to 8,145. Daily religious services had been attended by 9,150 people. In addition, Green and his wife had visited the sick and given food baskets to needy families. Hundreds of turkey dinners had been served at Thanksgiving and Christmas. During this period, Saturday night religious services were led by Southern Methodist University students and Sunday services by students from

Southwestern Baptist Theological Seminary.[21]

By this time, a mission pattern was developing. Most men who needed lodging were allowed to stay two or three nights at a small price. Those who exhibited special commitment to change were permitted to stay longer. The most common jobs they landed were as painters and carpenters. If Green smelled whiskey on anyone's breath, he was immediately kicked out. Approximately sixty rooms were occupied by these paying customers, who provided about two-thirds of the income needed to operate the hotel. Apparently, on only one occasion did Green have to call the police—when an inebriated man refused to leave and began pushing him. The police arrived and beat the man terribly.[22]

With the dawning of the 1950s, one of the most flamboyant figures in the story of Union Gospel Mission of Tarrant County began volunteering to help the homeless in ways that would benefit and publicize the mission for years. Bill Smith, better known as "Major Bill," had a colorful background. Born and raised in Checotah, Oklahoma, he had joined the Army Air Corps in World War II, flying numerous B-17 missions over Europe. On his thirty-third mission, the bombardier was hit. Smith was credited with saving his life, receiving shrapnel wounds in an arm in the process, and he was grounded as a result. He left the Air Force as a major, having received the Distinguished Flying Cross and Purple Heart. Following the war, he became Public Information Officer at Carswell Air Force Base in Fort Worth.

Major Bill also struggled with alcoholism, a condition he partly attributed to his war experiences. He eventually hit bottom and wound up on skid row, living from drink to drink. In 1953 he found himself at Union Gospel Mission of Tarrant County, was converted, and credited the mission with saving his life. His own experiences helped him identify with those who struggled daily just to hold their lives together.

Within a few years, Smith became a salesman for a Fort Worth meat company and also entered the music business, becoming a songwriter and record producer. In short order he was doing remarkably well. In 1961 he produced "Peanuts" by Rick and the Keens, and the next year the megahit "Hey, Baby!" by Bruce Channel, which went to the top of the charts. Then, just eleven months later, he had a second number-one hit, "Hey, Paula," and the next year produced "The Last Kiss," which became one of the biggest songs requested by teenagers in the history of radio.[23]

Royalties for these records gave him income that he shared liberally with Union Gospel Mission of Tarrant County. A chaplain at the mission said, "Bill had a very flamboyant side to him. He used his flamboyance to raise funds, then he would refunnel those funds to the poor." He added that although Bill "sometimes preached, most of his work was one-on-one with those on the street. He often went to the '40-ounce tree' at Lancaster and Riverside Drive to minister to alcoholics drinking from large bottles of beer" and did so "with a humble style that allowed him to talk to people on their level without getting down on their level." His son remembered the night Bill came home without any shoes. He had given them away.[24]

His commitment to these wayward souls led one man to speak of him in poetry:

*It's Tuesday night in Texas,*
*and the sun is going down.*

*A cloud descends and rain begins,*
*as lights go on downtown.*

*Honky-tonks and bar rooms blaze with music,*
*smoke, and song*

*While in the cold, wet alleyways,*
*discarded souls hang on.*

*A mission opens up its doors, and slowly*
*wandering in*

*Are the people no one else adores,*
*in clothes of other men;*

*Their thin-soled shoes a shuffle make,*
*they step in for a meal*

*And reach out for a bowl of soup*
*with hands too numb to feel.*


*And all around the table every*
*bloodshot eye is closed.*

*They bow their heads in thanks . . .*
*for what blessings? Heaven knows.*

*A high-pitched voice leads out in prayer,*
*a smiling soldier stands*

*And speaks to God just like a friend,*
*with upward reaching hands.*


*He prays for all the broken dreams,*
*for languished, lonely lives,*

*For all the men who've lost their way,*
*their children and their wives,*

*For all the burdened, broken souls*
*enslaved in Satan's snare,*

*And for the rest of us too good,*
*too comfortable to care.*[25]


Major Bill called the down-and-outers "street people" and would say, "You have to've had a home to be homeless." Many times Bill would arrive at the mission in the middle of the night with an armload of diapers and medicine. He never forgot the time a man handed him a handkerchief with a silver dollar tied inside it and told him, "This is so I will know I'm worth something." To Bill Smith, every person was worth something, and he devoted much of his life to showing it. His hope for a day shelter, while not realized in his lifetime, would one day become reality. When he died in 1994 at age 72, his funeral procession passed in front of the mission. People lined the sidewalk and placed their hands over their hearts. One man saluted.[26]

Early in the 1960s, Brother Roger Florence of Samuels Avenue Assembly of God church was mission superintendent, and two of his young church members were an important part of its daily life. Martha Athley, seventeen, and her little sister, Verna, thirteen, volunteered in the office and prayer room. They could rent out rooms as cheaply as one dollar a night or find a supplicant a free cot in the basement. They were used to drunkards and not afraid to deal with them but kept a wooden club behind the door just in case trouble arose. They were not allowed upstairs, except on the elevator. Nor were they permitted in the basement. If someone needed assistance going downstairs, Steve, the cook, was enlisted.[27]

"Some men stay a night, some stay a long time," said Verna. "I enjoy it here. You're doing something for people." She already knew how to make an effective appeal. "We need all kinds of things down here . . . dishes, clothing, furniture. The only help we get is from friends in the public or from the superintendent's own pocket."[28]

In 1963 a Baptist minister named Ewell Humphreys began what would be years of preaching and service at Union Gospel Mission of Tarrant County. He had some rewarding experiences that shed light on the mission's ministry. One Sunday, before Humphreys preached at the afternoon service, a young man was giving his testimony when a well-dressed man entered the mission and sat down. Humphreys thought little of it until two days later when Superintendent George Williams called him and said, "Come read this letter I received." The writer, after identifying himself, said that he had recently lost his job in Dallas. His wife left him. He decided that there was no worthwhile future for him. "I did not want to live," he confessed. He bought a .38-caliber pistol, loaded it, put it in his pocket, and was ready to end his life.

Outside the mission June 3, 1962.
Courtesy *Fort Worth Star-Telegram* collection,
Special Collections, the University of Texas at
Arlington Library, Arlington, Texas.

The Chamber of Commerce Beautification Committee
sponsored a spruce-up in May of 1963.
Courtesy *Fort Worth Star-Telegram* collection,
Special Collections, the University of Texas at
Arlington Library, Arlington, Texas.

"I drove around and came toward Fort Worth. Stopping at a red light, I heard singing and saw a sign 'Union Gospel Mission.' For some reason, I parked and went in." He said he heard a young man speaking about what the Lord meant to him. "Then the preacher spoke about Jesus, how much he loves us, even sinners, and gave his life and shed his blood to save us. I went back to Dallas, put the gun away, got on my knees and prayed to this God." His life soon turned around. "There is a good chance my wife and I will get back together. My heart is happy. I am saved by the grace of God. Thank God for Union Gospel Mission."[29]

One afternoon, after preaching at the mission, Humphreys invited people to come forward and accept Jesus Christ. A man, probably in his mid-sixties, came down the aisle, took Humphreys's hand and said, "Preacher, you said God loves all of us. I just got out of prison six months ago. I killed two men and am a drunkard. Do you mean God loves me?" Humphreys said, "Yes he does. What is your name?"

"Ivory Morten," he responded. "But people call me Soapy." When Humphreys told him to get on his knees and pray with him, Soapy confessed, "I don't know how." Humphreys told him to say simply, "Lord, help me." So Soapy leaned forward and put his hands on the concrete floor. Tears rolled down his face and fell onto his hands as he prayed, "Lord, can you help me?" Said Humphreys, "Soapy was saved."[30]

About a month later, Humphreys received a letter from Soapy. Placed inside the folded letter were six dollars. Soapy wrote that he had found a good job in Grand Prairie and had been told that he was to give one-tenth of his earnings to the Lord's work. The previous week he had been paid sixty dollars. He said, "I am sending you six dollars for your church."[31]

Sometimes there were surprises. One day, at the close of Humphreys's sermon, a man came forward and asked: "What do I need to do?" Humphreys told him: "Get rid of the bottle." Hearing that, the man reached up his coat sleeve, pulled out a big wine bottle and threw it across the room. It bounced all the way to the wall but never broke. Humphreys said, "Let us pray."[32]

On another afternoon, Humphreys was ministering in the city jail when a prisoner said "Hi, Brother Humphreys." "How do you know me?" asked Humphreys. The man said, "From Union Gospel Mission. I've been off of drugs for six months now." Humphreys said, "How long have you been here?" The man answered, "Six months."[33]

The Athley sisters and Ewell Humphrey were part of the traditional role and ministry the mission had lived out for years—taking drunks and drug addicts off the street, proclaiming the saving Gospel of Jesus Christ to them, feeding them and providing a place to spend the night. In the meantime, the area around the mission had become seedier and seedier. It had never been upscale. Planted in the midst of Hell's Half Acre, it had long been associated with skid row—flophouses, prostitutes, honky-tonks, vagrants. Union Gospel Mission of Tarrant County was one of several rescue efforts in that part of town.

That was about to change. Tarrant County officials were preparing to build a new convention center in the area that would serve two purposes. Not only would it provide large, needed meeting space and bring conventions to town, but it would also cause the rundown remnants of Hell's Half Acre to be torn down and lead to major urban renewal. For $5,200,000 the county bought all the property it needed. Plans moved quickly, and by February 10, 1965, the entire convention center site was to be vacated. Union Gospel Mission of Tarrant County barely escaped the wrecking ball. Sitting on the edge of the site to be cleared, it would be spared, but because it was one of the only missions left in the area, it would soon have huge demands placed on it.[34]

That February, crowding reached unprecedented levels as people flooded into the mission. All one hundred beds were filled, and sixty more bunks were stacked high. They, too, were soon occupied. George Williams, who was now superintendent, told a reporter that, in addition to these beds, pallets were spread on the floors, because "We don't turn anybody away." And since there was no room left at the city jail, police brought vagrants to the mission, exacerbating the problem. "There's getting to be no space for the wino," said Williams, "but we're not going to turn these men away." The mission "staff" even set up beds in the chapel near a sign that proclaimed: "It's Later Than You Think." The staff was composed of several mission employees paid with three meals a day, a place to sleep, first choice of clothes that had been contributed, and a daily sack of tobacco. To accommodate the crowd, men even repainted bedsteads that had come from dormitories at Arlington State College years earlier and placed them alongside army surplus cots in the basement. So jammed together were all these beds that a person could barely walk between them. And making matters worse was rainwater from a gutter pouring through a crack in the building.[35]

In March, conditions worsened. Cold, damp nights caused large numbers of men to seek shelter. By the end of the month, mission food was running low, with the meat supply good for only one more day. There was barely enough room to feed the men, and the meals were spartan. Each man was to get two meals a day—coffee, bread, and gravy for breakfast, and rice, beans, or soup in the evening. Chicken necks, when meat companies cleaned out freezers and donated them, were considered a delicacy with rice. Conditions led one newspaper to say the mission resembled a "displaced persons camp." There were no more mattresses for extra beds. "We had a $211 gas bill last month. We're running $100 to $200 in debt. We got more bills than we got money," said George Williams. "Every two or three days we see a definite upsurge in the men coming here. Some of them are sick. But we provide a place to get them off the street."[36]

And the next month did not promise to be better. Every April, the mission experienced a 25 percent increase in population as "snow-birds"—men who had come south for the winter—headed back north and stopped off in Fort Worth. Since the railroad just across the street brought most of them to town, the mission was the logical place to stay. Making matters even more challenging, word had also come that a bar, driven out of the convention center area, was moving in next door. Battling alcohol was tough enough without that development.[37]

Somehow the mission managed to meet these challenges and, as Christmas approached that year, was the recipient of an impressive, for-ty-two-foot-wide new sign. At a special event to dedicate it, Mayor Willard Barr, Superintendent George Williams, and incoming president of the mission board Rev. John F. Elliot of Calvary Presbyterian Church spoke.[38]

Coinciding with this celebration was the announcement of big plans for Christmas Day. Superintendent Williams would speak at 11:30 that morning, followed by the distribution of Christmas gifts and a 4:00 p.m. worship service led by John Elliot. Then at 5:00 p.m., three hundred persons would eat a turkey dinner donated by W. B. LaCava, outgoing president of the board. George Williams was scheduled to speak once more at 7:30 that evening.[39]

The months ahead brought increased demands on the mission as more and more homeless, destitute people found their way to its doors. The building was so full that house-hold goods were being stacked in the chapel. In August 1966, an electrical fire put even more strain on the budget and led to borrowing money that was to be repaid in monthly installments. These days were tough, and Superintendent Williams made one plea after another for financial support. As usual, he had a strong case. By November, he could say that in the previous month alone, the mission had served 9,589 meals, provided 2,281 beds, taken six-ty-nine people to hospitals, run 140 errands for residents, prayed with fifty-seven of them, and provided 876 pieces of clothing.[40]

And of the mission building, he could say:

[It] Is not the *highest building*, in Fort Worth, but the result of the business carried on inside reaches into heaven, and all who will, may ascend to the throne of the most high.

Is not a *bank*, but inside men have received riches this world knows not of. It has no safety deposit boxes to rent, but all are offered a place free for the safe-keeping of their soul (their most precious possession) for all eternity.

Is not a *hospital*, but it has a delivery room where men have been born again and delivered from the power of sin.

Is not a *beauty parlor*, but inside wrecked lives are made beautiful by the One who is altogether lovely.

Is not a *mountain* with a cool spring of water, but here men drink from the spring of living water and never thirst again.

Is not the *United Nations building*, but inside men meet the Prince of Peace and receive the Peace of God which passeth all understanding.

Is not a *hotel*, but one can get a shower, shave, meal, change of clothing, and a good night's rest for their weary body in a good clean bed supplied by the Son of God.[41]

As another Christmas drew near that year, George Williams spoke of "the men who have found Christ as the strength of their lives, the men who have turned their back on drink, the sick men who have found here a place of healing, the needy families who have found here help for their homes, the traveler who was strengthened and guided on his way; men, women and children." The increasing number of community organizations expanding the mission's resources was also impressive—from John Peter Smith Hospital, Tarrant County social services, Salvation Army, American Red Cross, and Travelers Aid Society to the Veterans Administration, the Fort Worth Police Department, the District Attorney's office, and the county's public school systems.[42]

Even more telling was the growing number of people being helped. In November 1966, 12,070 meals had been served, 2,673 beds provided, seventy-five people taken to hospitals, fifty sick beds provided, more than nine hundred articles of clothing, and 150 pieces of furniture distributed. But these were more than simply numbers. A young professional man had spent several weeks at the mission until, once again, he was able to function on his own. Another man whose family had been helped by the mission wrote: "Brother Williams, you have made a very difficult situation a pleasant experience." George Williams sincerely hoped that "you of Fort Worth will consider this a part of our Christmas gift to you, for we know of no greater way of telling our city and the county of how much we love those who are our friends and doing the work we are set aside for, as you would want to have it done."[43]

But financially this remained a tough time for the mission, with needs far outstripping resources. So in February 1967, George Williams explained the basic purpose of Union Gospel Mission of Tarrant County and the conditions of the people it was serving. In his letter to current and prospective donors, he reminded them that the mission dealt primarily with men. Families, women, and children were served in emergency situations and then referred to agencies better equipped to meet their needs. In working with men, he said that there was one thing that always should be remembered: "All of our men have a problem. All of them in some way, to some degree, are sick when they come to the mission. They would not come if they were

not." Their problems varied from day to day. "Today it might have been an accident or a fight. Tomorrow it may be sickness or frustration. The next day it might be spiritual or emotional or mental. All on the same man and perhaps within a week."[44]

The approach to a problem was simple, said Williams. "We take care of it. . . . Whatever we do is done at that particular time for that particular man the best way we know. . . ." For that reason, the mission did not have a long list of "'do's and don'ts,' for if we began to handicap ourselves with rules that would keep us from serving the men, we would be defeating what our conception of the love of God towards men should be, for he said to forgive seventy times seven."[45]

This did not mean that there were no rules whatsoever. For instance, men were expected to be "quiet" and "decent" toward one another at the mission. And of course, one of the rules was that no liquor bottles were permitted. However, since no one could dictate to men when they left the premises, another rule stipulated that those who wanted to visit some bars after the evening worship service were required to wait one hour past the bars' closing times before they could be readmitted to the mission. "This may explain why sometimes men are standing outside the mission, late at night," explained Williams. "Men coming in late who have not been drinking and the stranger off the road are handled differently."[46]

And to those who might have thought that mission residents were basically lazy, Williams made clear that very few of them were able to work. "In fact, I do not know of any who are able to hold jobs who use the mission to dodge work." As evidence, he reminded this audience that between one and two hundred men every month went from the mission to jobs and that hundreds of hours were spent in "occasional" jobs through employment agencies.[47]

He was also honest about shortcomings. "The mission property is not as neat as I would

Dr. Paul Campbell, 1971.
Courtesy *Fort Worth Star-Telegram* collection,
Special Collections, the University of Texas at
Arlington Library, Arlington, Texas.

like to see it. Our 'Thank You Letters' do not always get out on time. " The staff, he admitted, was not always efficient, and their "behavior patterns will vary greatly." But even all of this was used as part of a fundraising plea: "Many of these things could be changed, and perhaps greatly, if our income were only more adequate." The appeal, he continued, "is to your heart."[48]

By this time the Auxiliary of Union Gospel Mission of Tarrant County had become an important arm of its ministry. And it had grown dramatically. Women from many denominational backgrounds, drawn to the good work of the mission, had joined the auxiliary—so many, in fact, that the auxiliary divided into two groups that met monthly. One was meeting in the home of Mrs. Elliot on Jennings Avenue, and the other in Mrs. Peter Kaspick's home in Everman. Some women who could not attend

either meeting worked at home on special projects.

Both groups had a common purpose: helping the mission with their work, prayers, and money. At every meeting they collected a love offering. They also took on common projects—making quilts, pillowcases, and nightshirts, and hemming sheets. "There is something for any woman to do if she wants to help the mission," said Mrs. Elliot. "When they clean out their closets, many women find articles that would help us. We especially need thin, old sheet blankets, maybe too thin to use on a bed but just the thing to line the quilts we make." In November 1967 alone, the mission fed almost nine thousand people. It was also maintaining a well-stocked store that constantly needed resupplying with furniture, stoves, clothing, shoes, dishes, and household utensils. These items helped families burned out of their homes as well as those sent to the mission by welfare agencies. Children were even brought to the mission to be outfitted for school.[49]

"We always seem to be having emergencies," said Mrs. Elliot. "The boiler blew out . . . costing one thousand dollars to replace. The auxiliary gave money instead of the socks they usually donate for the men at Christmas and also gave the proceeds from their bazaar. Everything we make goes to the mission. We don't keep anything."[50]

In the summer of 1968, the nation was in tremendous turmoil, trying to deal with the assassinations of Senator Robert Kennedy and Martin Luther King Jr. Protesters were in the streets, clamoring for an end of the Vietnam War, as well as the need to address poverty and civil rights. But on the home front, Union Gospel Mission of Tarrant County's ministry steadily remained what it had always been—a haven that helped those in need and ministered to the desperate on the fringes of society who were dealing with daily hurts.

Paul Campbell was now director of the mission, doing everything in his power to address the growing day-to-day needs of his flock. There were many small victories. A man named Solomon Jennings was given free lodging and food until he landed a job paying four dollars an hour. And J. E. Garrett, after a short stay, landed a one-hundred-dollar-a-week job at American Manufacturing Company. Others were finding short-term work at twelve dollars to fourteen dollars a day. All were reasons to rejoice. Especially encouraging was the return of a twenty-two-year-old young man who had left the mission to head for California. He came back with a confession that he and two companions had used a gasoline credit card that was not theirs. Paul Campbell knew that this man did not have to return and, upon hearing that he wanted to sell his car to make restitution to Humble Oil Company, worked with him to clear his name.[51]

Christmas 1968 was one of the mission's best. More than four hundred meals were provided on Christmas Day, and many young people who had volunteered during the previous summer returned to celebrate and serve. They donated not only food and clothing but also money. One young man made an extra-special gift that day. Having won a Mustang convertible in a contest, he sold it to raise money for his education and then gave a generous portion of the proceeds to Union Gospel Mission of Tarrant County.[52]

As the 1960s came to a close, Union Gospel Mission of Tarrant County lost one of its most dedicated servants. Col. C. S. Elliot, who had been a board member since the 1930s and its chairman since 1966, died at the age of eighty-six. Born in a frontier environment, he had tried, but was too young, to join Theodore Roosevelt's Rough Riders in the Spanish-American War. He went on to serve in both world wars, to run a real estate company, learn several foreign languages, work with a number of service organizations, and become a leader in his church. His was a life that witnessed tremendous changes—born in the days of wagon trains and living to see Neil Armstrong walk on the moon.

But Colonel Elliot's greatest legacy could well have been the love and labor he gave to Union Gospel Mission of Tarrant County. He had become part of not only the fabric but also the very foundation of the mission. He had personified Jesus's teaching: "In as much as ye have done it unto the least of these, ye did it unto me," said Paul Campbell. "It is no wonder that Colonel Elliot and I became such close friends. We thought alike, worked alike, and had the same goals regarding unfortunate men who needed a lot of help—those who were cold, hungry, far from home." C.S. Elliot was a prime example of the dedicated, faith-filled people without whom the mission would likely have been far less effective.[53]

In the spring of 1970, Union Gospel Mission of Tarrant County announced its new officers and board members. The new president was Odell McBrayer; the vice president, William T. Read. J. W. Capps served as second vice president, Ray Anderson as secretary, and G. E. Mahan as treasurer. Board members were Dr. John F. Elliot, James A. Gordon, Ewell J. Humphreys, W. B. LaCava, Allen H. Sagar, Charles F. Tegethoff, Robert T. Welborn, Dr. Paul Campbell, Malcolm J. Haile, Rev. Waymore Goldberg, and Rev. J. H. Williams. On the mission's advisory board were Johnnie Johnson, A. B. Sammons, William E. Mitseh Jr., W. F. Lilley, Cato Hightower, US Representative Jim Wright, R. D. Ermin, and T. E. Graham.[54]

That same year one of the mission's most interesting volunteers also arrived. Mission chaplain Warren Ambrose was having difficulty finding people to preach at the numerous worship services. He invited Bill Russell, better known as Brother Bill, which led to a preaching ministry that would continue for decades. Brother Bill, who would eventually complete two degree programs at Criswell Bible Institute in Dallas, was a flamboyant presence. His sermons, while varying in details, consistently contained Christian themes he considered

Dr. Bill Russell preaches at Union Gospel Mission of Tarrant County chapel. Courtesy *Fort Worth Star-Telegram* collection, Special Collections, the University of Texas at Arlington Library, Arlington, Texas.

basic: rest for the weary, food for the hungry, comfort for the heart, light for those in darkness, restoration for the wayward, salvation for the lost, peace for those in turmoil, joy for the gloomy, hope for the despondent, and drink for the thirsty. Some weeks he preached twenty times.[54]

Tom Redwine, who became a board member in 1971, described the mission at that time as being primarily a place to sober up drunks. And that was not the worst of it. Funding was low and there was limited staffing, so residents tended to manage the place. Several of the long-term residents banded together and ran the place to their advantage. It was a rough time. Some men were given the responsibility of being floor managers at night, a role that, on more than one occasion, became impossible to carry out. In fact, so violent had the situation become that some of these floor managers were found murdered near the Trinity River. Security and safety

issues intensified, and by 1973 the mission was seriously strapped for money, with only a small pool of donors left and no full-time superintendent. In fact, board members were taking turns, volunteering in shifts, to take men in off the street. They even shared leading devotional services.[55]

Despite all these problems, Paul Campbell could feel good about what was happening to the downtown area around the mission, claiming that "the saloons and flop houses are gone forever. Over 100 years of this life is over. Before long a beautiful water garden built by the Amon Carter Foundation will grace the space directly in front of the Mission Building." But he was also preparing to retire, announcing that his last day as superintendent would be January 15, 1973. He and his wife would be moving to Bonham, Texas.

The Rev. Sealy Smith stepped in as superintendent for the next few months until his successor, Charley Byers, arrived that summer. Charley brought with him a colorful past. "I was quite a drinkin' boy myself once," he admitted. A former truck driver and used-car salesman, according to rumor he had also been a horse thief and was headed for the pen. He showed up at a lunch of the Full Gospel Businessmen's Fellowship with one of his hands crushed from a recent accident. At the lunch he prayed for the hand to be healed, claimed that it was, and called it a miracle. "I used to hang around with a bunch of ol' drunk toughies, but one morning I pulled up and there they all were, sitting together praying," he recalled. "I decided they had something I didn't and I decided to find the Lord. Two weeks later I was asked if I'd like to help out here." He began as a part-time mission worker, but by the summer of 1973, was named executive director. "I'd never even been to a place like this," he admitted, "but I've been here ever since."[56]

Byers, who never finished grammar school, grew up on Fort Worth's North Side and served in World War II. He had been exposed to some religious training while his father was superintendent of a Baptist church Sunday school, but had abandoned religion much of his adulthood and lived what he called the "hard life."[57]

In his first year as director of the mission, Charley provided a revealing description of its work. During July 1974 it had provided 2,931 meals to hungry men, beds for 544 transients for up to three nights each, housed an average of thirteen staff members each day, and rented rooms to twenty men every night. "When a man comes to us," said Charley, "he is usually broke, out of a job, often has a hangover, and needs clothing, food, and shelter." The mission would give a man two meals and a bed, and wash his clothes or give him new ones. "We are especially interested in men who are trying to quit drinking," he continued. "If a man indicates that he sincerely wants help, we will put him on the staff, put him in a two-man room . . . provide

Charley Byers
Union Gospel Mission of Tarrant County collection.

three meals a day, a clean wardrobe, and put him to work. . . . Our primary concern is that the men come to know Jesus as Savior and claim for themselves the power of the Holy Spirit." Charley, like the director before him, was persuaded that "only Jesus can create an ex-alcoholic."[58]

As usual, operations were limited by a tight budget. Expenses were approximately $3,000 a month. One-third of that came from room rentals and chapel worship service offerings. The remainder had to be raised from those Charley called "God's people." Most of these gifts were in the ten- or twenty-dollar range. "Occasionally," said Charley, "God will send someone with larger contributions, but these are rare."[59]

What a mix of men found their way to the mission! Charley used the word *variety*. Some were fugitives from justice; some, he admitted, were "just plain running. A few of these have found peace at the mission." Several had come straight from the penitentiary, having served more than a quarter century behind bars and bringing with them heartbreaking stories.[60]

Ex-cons were not the only arrivals with sad stories. One day in 1974 a fifty-four-year-old, one-legged man appeared at the mission. His was quite a tale. He had grown up in Fort Worth, married, fathered children, and held a government job for fourteen years. And then, as Charley described it, "Satan came into his life and he started drinking; just a little at first, and then more and more." It reached a point where his lunch pail, instead of food, held a bottle of liquor. After losing his job, home, car, and family, he began sleeping in missions, alleys, and parks. He eventually caught a freight train across the Arizona desert but managed to fall under it and almost lose a leg. Believing he was about to die, he began crawling beside the tracks and later claimed it was on that crawl that he found God. After about three hours of this misery, an engineer on a passing train spotted him and called the local sheriff, who got him to a hospital where his life was saved, but not his leg.[61]

Not long afterward he arrived at Union Gospel Mission of Tarrant County with what Charley Byers described as "a Bible and the happiest smile I have ever seen on a man's face." He said he hoped to work at the mission because he wanted to be in the Lord's house. Charley put him to work painting, cooking, and washing dishes. He became an active participant in worship services, often testifying. "It was wonderful," said Charley, "because he could talk these men's language. We praise the Lord for the blessing this man has been to us."[62]

But his time at the mission would be short. He lived only a few months after arriving. Charley expressed the feelings of many: "Our friend went on to meet the Lord, the very place he and I had been talking about." But though his physical being was gone, his presence was not.

"His friendship and his fellowship seem to still linger in the mission," said Charley. "He was such a great blessing and he still seems so very close."[63]

Union Gospel Mission of Tarrant County had some amazing success stories during these years—some with people who had experienced almost unbelievable tragedies. No better example could be found than a man who showed up in rags at the mission's front door, drunk, dirty, unshaven. Even to mission workers his story was shocking. As an eighteen-year-old, he hunted down and murdered a man for molesting and killing his nine-year-old sister. Sentenced to fifty years in the penitentiary, he was finally paroled at age fifty-five. He returned home, and after he had been there only one week, his entire family—mother, father, and sisters—were killed when their automobile was hit by a train.[64]

These events were overwhelming. He began drinking heavily and arrived at the mission in bad shape. After a bath, a shave, and being given some clean clothes, he asked what he could do to help. For one dollar a day, Charley put him to work washing dishes and then, to his surprise, learned that this newcomer was an excellent cook. He had cooked for years in the penitentiary. Over the next months, with God's help, this grieving man, while cooking some of the best meals the mission had served in years, began rebuilding his life and envisioning a future for himself. He landed a job as assistant manager of a leading Fort Worth restaurant, and with deep gratitude left the mission to begin his new life. "He came to visit me a few days ago," Charley said. "He was clean, well groomed, and well dressed, and had a look of happiness that can come only from the Lord. He made it clear to me that his stay at the Union Gospel Mission had pointed him to a life of usefulness and happiness."[65]

# CHAPTER SIX

A snapshot of the mission in the mid-1970s would show a staff of eleven or twelve men who, for one dollar a day, cleaned the premises, operated the kitchen, cooked the meals, washed dishes, and did whatever else needed doing—sometimes working eighteen hours a day. Charley Byers boasted that nine out of eleven of these men "have surrendered to our Lord and Savior." Some of them, he admitted, "are not a pretty sight when they come here, but once we see the love of our Lord getting through to them, they become very beautiful to work with."[1]

Some of the rules of the mission during this period revealed a lot about it, such as: "No liquor on premises. When bottles are found, the man has the choice of pouring out the bottle and staying or taking the bottle with him and leaving. If found drinking on the premises . . . they are asked to leave." Another rule was "Men are accepted in all conditions. We put drunks to bed to sober up . . . the only limitation is their refusal of aid or unbearable behavior. We accept any man as he is. We do not fuss. We call upon the Lord and then minister with what we have. We are not perfect, and if we fail with a man, we call upon the Lord and try again."[2]

Charley Byers and the mission seemed to be a good fit. "This is the greatest thing I've ever done," he said, "and it's a job most people won't have." By December 1974, Byers needed all the optimism he could muster. The old boiler, which had been in the building since it was built in the midtwenties, had finally and

permanently failed. Its replacement cost $8,000. City inspectors paid a visit, and they wanted the elevator condemned and the water and electrical systems updated. Even more troubling, they expressed the hope that the mission could be moved to another location. Board president Odell McBrayer, a local attorney, worked with the city to slow things down and find ways to keep the mission functioning. On Christmas Day Byers announced that

Mission director Charley Byers, 1975.
*Courtesy Fort Worth Star-Telegram collection, Special Collections, the University of Texas at Arlington Library, Arlington, Texas.*

Exterior of Union Gospel Mission of Tarrant County at 1514 Houston Street, 1971.
Courtesy *Fort Worth Star-Telegram* collection, Special Collections, the University of
Texas at Arlington Library, Arlington, Texas.

with $3,000 in hand, he had committed to raise the remaining $5,000 for the new boiler within ninety days. "In the year and a half I've been here, we have never solicited for money or asked for anything," he said. "The money, what we need, just comes. Sometimes at the end of a month I may have $16, but we have never failed to pay a bill on time."[3]

On that cold Christmas Day, the mission was housing about 275 residents who would most likely be there until warm weather arrived. Each man was given a room or a bunk, a mattress, sheet, and pillow—but no blankets. "We just don't have them," said Byers. "On the milder nights, I've given the men two and three sheets to cover them, but some nights have been so cold they just sat up all night in the chapel. It was too cold to sleep."[4]

Byers was both caring and realistic about those he was trying to help. Admitting that most people considered the mission little more than a flophouse, he said, "I guess that's true, in a way. But no one else cares for these people. We get referrals from the hospital, the jail, from United Way agencies, and the churches send them." Some were "just ugly," he confessed. "No one else will put up with them. When they're not drunk, they're mean and obnoxious. But we'll take care of them."[5]

Despite the difficulties, Byers seemed pleased with the mission's performance. Although he was the only full-time employee, residents could earn a dollar a day for helping out. Several had saved their money to purchase wanted items. In addition, four men over seventy-five years old were provided room and

J. T., chief cook for the mission, August 1975.
Courtesy *Fort Worth Star-Telegram* collection,
Special Collections, the University of Texas at
Arlington Library, Arlington, Texas.

board for just sixty dollars a month because, as Byers well knew, they could not afford to live anywhere else. He also wanted it known that in that year, 1974, the mission had served more than 90,000 free meals at an average cost of less than a nickel apiece. Local stores, as well as meat and produce businesses, donated good food that they were unable to sell. Bakeries gave broken or stale loaves. "It's been a long time since we've failed to have at least three items on the plate," Byers boasted.[6]

That same year, because of obvious needs in Fort Worth, the mission expanded to two new locations. An increasing number of troubled women and girls were showing up at the door. "Obviously we can't keep them here," Byers explained. "There is no place else for them to go. They come in here sometimes, own nothing in

the world but a man's shirt and a pair of pants. I mean nothing else. They are down and out and desperate." Responding to this problem, the mission established a women's home at 7315 Ewing Street. Bus station employees and police referred runaways as well as women thrown out by their families for becoming pregnant. "We kept one woman six months until her baby was born," recalled Byers. "Then her family agreed to take her back."[7]

A crisis of stranded, penniless families met a similar response. In September, as a way to begin addressing this growing problem, the mission purchased the property of the Baptist Rescue Mission at 1327 East Lancaster and converted it into a family center. Almost immediately a call came from Travelers Aid requesting help for a desperate family. A mother and father with twin, nine-month-old sons had been sleeping in their car in a park for five nights because they had run out of money and had nowhere to go. Byers learned that the family was on its way to Phoenix and set them up in the new family center. After eight days of work, the father had earned enough to continue the journey. Byers said, "We provide food, shelter, and medical attention as long as they need it." During the cold months of winter, many stranded families needed it.[8]

Byers initiated another important change. Previously, the policy of the mission had required men to attend a worship service in the chapel before they were allowed to eat. Byers reversed the order so that the men ate first and then attended chapel—if they chose to. "We have almost as many as ever," he claimed. "But there's no reason for a man who's sick and miserable to try and listen. He can't hear the message."[9]

By 1975, with the creation of the Fort Worth Water Gardens, the commitment of Fort Worth civic leaders to improve and even beautify the area around the mission became clear. Designed by Philip Johnson and John Burgee of

New York and given to the city by the Amon G. Carter Foundation, the Water Gardens filled an entire city block directly across the street from Union Gospel Mission of Tarrant County. Featuring large descending steps, waterfalls, and landscaped terraces, it became a quiet haven from the noise and bustle of downtown.[10]

Meanwhile, the Christ-centered work of the mission continued, largely through the energy and commitment of Charley Byers. He had a simple answer to the question of how the mission changed lives. "I have been asked by many people, 'Who supports the mission? Where does the money come from for the mission?'" Charley's response: "The only honest answer I have is—through our friend, Jesus." Again and again he proclaimed that "in spite of some smirks and even a few light laughters . . . we are supported by our friend Jesus."

He meant it and offered examples, telling of a well-known prominent Fort Worth citizen who, over a weekend, needed immediate help. Desperate, he contacted a man who identified himself simply as "a friend of Jesus"—he did not know it was Charley Byers—and received the assistance he needed. Around the same time, someone called to report a young mother sitting on the sidewalk, weeping, with a baby in her arms. Addressing the caller, Charley claimed, "Because of you being in the family of Jesus, he had you call us. . . . We went to help because we believe Jesus leads us." This young woman, ill and unable to work, had been evicted from her small apartment because she owed back rent. "But," said Charley, "our friend Jesus, through you, had already provided a bed, a bath, clothing, and food for this young mother and baby at the Union Gospel Mission. What a friend we have in Jesus!"

The 1977 year-end numbers indicated that these stories were multiplied many times. In that year alone, the mission had served more than 177,000 meals, provided lodging for 55,175 individuals with immediate needs and 4,491

people at the family center. In addition, almost seven hundred people had received transportation to and from local hospitals. At the same time, the mission was making a little money go a long way, claiming that a one-dollar donation would feed a man for a week or buy gas for ten trips to the hospital. "Hard to believe," went the pitch, "but true."

All these figures, of course, were more than numbers. They were real people with real life stories and real needs. Such was a man named J. T. Taylor who, in 1974, appeared at the mission with major problems. Suffering from a rare illness that affected his feet, J. T. could barely walk. Lonely and grieving over losing custody of his daughter, he found both assurance and medical assistance through the mission. In 1978, J. T. returned to the mission, this time with his daughter and in the role of assistant superintendent. With experience as a male nurse, he set up what he called a small "hospital room" to care for some of the sick, elderly residents. He waited on them day and night, prepared their food and administered their medicine. J. T. took no personal credit but thanked God for the opportunity he had been given to serve.

Despite its success stories, the mission faced continued challenges. One of these involved the Water Gardens next door—a city project to enhance that often-neglected part of downtown. Though beautiful, with water flowing from one level to another, and definitely an asset to the area, its proximity to the mission presented problems. "That's exactly where we don't need to be," lamented Charley Byers. "It's one of the closest places for winos to hide, and police are always picking them up lying in the shrubbery over there." In one instance, a wino had been stabbed in the Water Gardens, then had run across the street and collapsed in the lobby of the mission.[11]

By now, pressure was intensifying to find a way to relocate the mission. It had to function the best it could with what it had in the meantime. In the cold, early spring of 1978, freezing rain had forced enough people off the streets to overflow the facilities. Because of a fight the previous week, the basement was closed to avoid further incidents. The mission's two-dollar rooms were full. A bedraggled elderly man who was turned away protested, "But I'm sober!" He was told "Sorry, no room."[12]

Bill Lewis, an on-and-off resident for years, was typical of many who had found refuge there. For a while he had actually been an assistant director of the mission. "He just fell," said Charley Byers. "Bill got a dollar a day for working around here for about three years and then he went up to $25 a week as assistant director, and he really had the feeling he was doing something. But then he just went out and got drunk." Sitting in the auditorium that served as the mission's chapel, television room, and reception area, Lewis confessed, "I'm ashamed of myself." But then he backtracked. "No, I'm not. I'm not. You can't think like that." A nearby sign declared, "Unruly persons will be removed as necessary." As he spoke, some twenty men sat nearby in folding chairs, talking or silently waiting for the dinner bell. Lewis was philosophical about them. "I can never tell if they're thinking back to their childhood or if their mind is in outer space. You'd be surprised how many of these men have trades, though. But something happened. They stopped and gave up. But then, I can't say anything because I did the same thing."[13]

By this time, the condition of the mission was deteriorating noticeably. "This old building is nothing but an eyesore and probably would have come down a long time ago if it weren't a mission," Lewis claimed. He was probably right. The rooms needed paint. They still had nothing nicer than bare concrete floors. The smell of urine permeated the restrooms. The mission continued to rely on donations from individuals, churches, and grocers, and its small budget simply could not keep pace with all that needed to be done. It was a matter of priorities and first things first—helping the needy.[14]

Despite the obvious problems and limitations, Charley Byers remained optimistic and confident that he was doing what God called him to do. He knew the upsides and the downsides of his calling. "I've got a stack of letters from people thanking us for giving a baby a bed, keeping a family for a week, or just helping out someone. And that makes me feel real good," he admitted. "But then sometimes a guy'll try to cut me with a butter knife or a wine bottle, but then the next day he'll be in this office, just weeping, saying 'I'm sorry, Charley. I don't know what got into me.'"

In 1978, Byers and Lewis took time to describe to a reporter the kinds of men who were filling the mission. Byers said, "Some . . .come in here and want to fight or cut each other. Lately we've just had too many hippies on dope. Last month I had to get the police out here three times one night." Some were good men, he claimed—doctors and lawyers—but alcohol had brought them down. "There was one man—I used to go out every morning and pick him up from the alley back there. He'd had a good job with one of the airlines, a family, two Cadillacs. But he just got to drinkin' the booze."[15]

Lewis estimated that about eighty percent of residents were alcoholics and the rest had drug problems. "If I had the intelligence I would have written a book about this place—the comical parts, the sad parts—and it would have sold, I bet. . . . " He gave the mission a fitting moniker—a "survival kit"—and contended, "There is a great need for a place like this. It's good for a person that truly needs it but then you get some people who don't have any initiative and use it as a crutch." The reality was, he claimed, "You just have to deal with people and understand others and their problems. You've got to take the good with the bad, but technically there is no bad. You've got to find the good."[16]

# CHAPTER SEVEN

By August 1978, the *Star-Telegram* carried news that Union Gospel Mission would soon be razed and moved to a new location. Its new home: seven blocks east of downtown, on Lancaster Street. The mission's current property would be sold by the Fort Worth Development Corporation and the proceeds applied to the new facility. J. C. Pace, president of the Chamber Development Corporation, called the sale money "peanuts" compared to the cost of the new building. "We're a nonprofit corporation," he said, "interested in upgrading downtown Fort Worth." [1]

Word of the relocation came as no real surprise to Charley Byers, who had declared, "The old building is falling apart on us. It's in terrible shape. We've had to close the basement, which was our dormitory area, and we can't handle as many people." The previous year, as many as 250 people attended the mission's religious services. Now, because deteriorating conditions reduced the mission's useable space, attendance rarely reached one hundred. Obviously, something had to be done. [2]

Not surprisingly, despite the impending disruption, Byers was excited about the move. The new building would be "beautiful," he predicted, and not too far from downtown to help needy men and women. "People don't know what we do," he claimed. "They think all we do is take care of drunks." He was quick to point out that the mission now operated a family center in a two-story building next to the mission's future location. Battered wives as well as entire families with no place to go were housed there, although the accommodations were dilapidated. In addition, elderly men with small Social Security checks, "too sick to have any place else to go," could find both room and board at the mission for around sixty dollars a month. These men looked forward to the move for several reasons. For one thing, they would be separated from drunken transients staying on the first floor, who would be brought into the building through a separate entrance. In the new building these elderly men would be on the second floor, with rooms featuring patios. [3]

Even in its existing dreary situation, the mission continued to carry out a remarkable ministry. During the previous year, without help from United Way or public assistance of any kind, it had served 117,000 meals at less than five cents apiece. "They're not supported by anything but free-will donations and what they call 'faith,'" said J. C. Pace. But then he added, "Faith must be a pretty good means of support." Indeed it was. [4]

As head of the Chamber Development Corporation, Pace worked closely with three other members—H. B. "Babe" Fuqua, M. J. Neeley, and Clark Nowlin—to relocate Union Gospel Mission of Tarrant County. This was an influential foursome. Pace, in his role, helped set a number of downtown priorities and recruited others to help make them happen. Babe Fuqua was president of Fort Worth National Bank. Clark Nowlin and M. J. Neeley were well-known businessmen and civic leaders whose support

The old building at 1514 Houston being demolished. It would be replaced by a new mission building at 1331 East Lancaster.
Courtesy *Fort Worth Star-Telegram* collection, Special Collections, the University of Texas at Arlington Library, Arlington, Texas.

of any project was always invaluable. In fact, Texas Christian University's School of Business was named for M. J. Neeley.[5]

"We will be getting rid of the unsightly old building, but more importantly we will be providing better facilities for the mission," said J. C. Pace. Although "better facilities" were cited as being more important, the initial motivation, of course, was the desire to get rid of the "unsightly old building," an eyesore in the midst of planned downtown renovations. The mission's nearness to the Water Gardens, as well as to other areas slated for renewal, spurred civic leaders to seek a way to relocate it. Their offer: to build a new building in another location in exchange for the present property.[6]

Charles Tegethoff, a Catholic attorney chair-

ing the mission's board, indicated that downtown leaders were collecting money for the new building and that donations had come from foundations as well as individuals. "Some persons have made single donations of as much as $5,000," he said.[7]

In the meantime, Charley Byers continued to be surprised by some of the people who wound up at the mission. "There's one professional musician everybody in Texas would know if I would call his name, who is in here every once in a while." He sympathized with men who once led normal lives, who found themselves penniless, abandoned by families, and looking for the next drink. "I've had them die here," Byers lamented. "You go up to check on them and you find them just sitting there with a wine bottle

The men's building, before remodeling.
Union Gospel Mission of Tarrant County collection.

in their hand . . . leaned back against the wall."
Experience had turned him into a realist. "I
don't say we save a lot of them. We don't expect to. We realize when a man comes here, he
has to be in a lot of trouble." Byers had learned
how fragile life can be and how quickly people
could fall. He said, "You would just be surprised
at how many good men, intelligent men, are in
these back alleys drinking wine. Our job is to
get them out of the back alleys."[8]

What kept him going? It was more than his
$185-a-week salary. Sometimes former res-
idents came to see him, ones who had arrived
at the mission in terrible shape but, with God's
help, had managed to put their lives back together and return to their families. Also, said
Byers, "There may be a guy dying here, and he
says he is at peace with the Lord. These are the
things that make it worthwhile."[9]

While Byers's work in the old building con-

tinued, the new building was being erected on
property a few blocks east of downtown. "As our
new building gets taller and taller," said Charley early in 1979, "we just praise the Lord. We
here at the mission can see daily progress." By
the end of the year, with construction completed, Union Gospel Mission of Tarrant County
moved into its new home at 1331 East Lancaster.

Not only did the mission's location change,
but its effort to serve women was also in transition. Prior to the move, women were housed
in the rooms of a dilapidated hotel so seedy it
was nicknamed Skid Row Hotel. Right after the
move, the mission purchased an old nightclub
next door to the new facility. It was not an up-
grade from the hotel, however. The windows had
no screens, and mice and rats made themselves
at home. Two dedicated women ministered in
this setting: Dorothy Harmon, president of the
local Women's Aglow Fellowhip, worked with

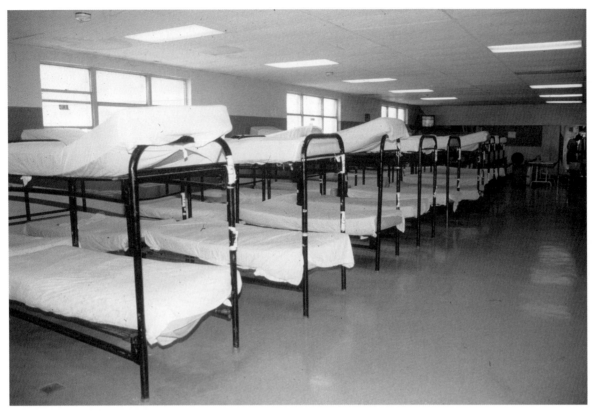

The dormitory in the men's building, before remodeling.
Union Gospel Mission of Tarrant County collection.

women referred to as "up and outers," while Myrtle Hardy, who had worked on the streets for years, served the "down and outers." The mission still had a long way to go, however, before it could give adequate help to women.[10]

Although Charley Byers helped the mission move to its new quarters, he would not be able to enjoy them for long. In 1980, he died of cancer. It was a big loss, and tributes came from numerous organizations and individuals. Charley had made a big impact. One of the finest tributes was from M. J. Neeley, who had played a pivotal role in creating the new building. "Charley Byers is the unforgettable man, the Union Gospel Mission is the unforgettable institution," he said. "His was an amazing accomplishment. He hung onto God's hand. He prayed for God's help . . . I believe that the star in Charley's crown is his reward for helping to

dispel the darkness of despair and admit the light of hope and faith into the hearts of those who came his way." Charley, he claimed, was "our *unforgettable friend.*"

To fill the gap, longtime board member Tom Redwine stepped in as interim director. It was a rough time in the life of the mission. Some of the men had been paroled from the criminal justice system and had ties to organized crime in Fort Worth. They were hard to manage and did pretty much as they pleased, resisting supervision and attempting to exert their own authority. To his amazement, Redwine even discovered that his office phone and the boardroom had been bugged.[11]

Such were some of the conditions when Bob Scott arrived in July 1981, as full-time superintendent—the position now called executive administrator. Whereas Charley Byers had run

When the mission ran out of beds during cold weather, homeless men found a warm spot on the chapel carpet.
Courtesy *Fort Worth Star-Telegram* collection, Special Collections, the University of Texas at Arlington Library, Arlington, Texas.

the mission with exuberant determination and the benefit of a life experience that enabled him to identify with those he helped, Bob Scott was a seasoned administrator. After serving in the Pacific in World War II and completing postgraduate studies in clinical psychology, he worked for several large corporations in medical-related fields. He then entered social work, gaining experience in alcohol recovery programs, and served a stint as a nursing-home administrator. Obviously, he came to Union Gospel Mission of Tarrant County with valuable experience. Soon after arriving at the mission, he developed its first organized bookkeeping system. Bob Scott was a low-key, bottom-line person who saw as one of his primary tasks the creation of a sense of order and predictability in the mission's daily life.[12]

He also took time to spell out, in a clear, concise statement, why Union Gospel Mission

of Tarrant County existed and what it was created to do. The goal of its founders, he claimed, was "to alleviate the pain of being hungry and in need, and to bring those persons to Christ." He continued, "We help those men, women, and children who appear to be in immediate need of shelter, food, baths, clean clothes, and a clean safe bed. And we do this," he said, "without making them fill out countless forms and answering questions to 'prove the facts' of their need. The fact that they are at our door appears to be highly adequate proof."[13]

Scott described how the mission dealt with these people. They were immediately told of the availability of the chapel and about the chaplain staff. Most admissions occurred after 5:00 p.m., and by 9:30 the men's dormitory was usually filled. Although the building was locked at 11:00 p.m., a latecomer could be admitted at any hour with the understanding that he might

Lenora Keffer, whose husband lost his job, with three of her five children—all staying at the Women's Shelter in 1986.
Courtesy *Fort Worth Star-Telegram* collection, Special Collections, the University of Texas at Arlington Library, Arlington, Texas.

wind up sleeping on the lobby floor. Scott underscored that "All of these things are offered without charge and without subjective judgment of fault."[14]

Mornings were full. Bathing and dressing began around 5:30 a.m., and breakfast was served at 6:00. Then the men who were able left for various labor pools or with contractors who needed extra help. Others were given in-house chores, and those who needed medical attention were taken to a clinic. Most men stayed only a few days; others remained longer, until it was apparent that they had become spiritually and financially restored to the point where they could leave and take on full-time employment. Some men, those who showed strong commitment to improving themselves, were invited to become part of the in-house staff. These were men who gave service in exchange for room and board and minor gratuities. "It is truly a marvel," said Scott. As space permitted, these residents could move to small upstairs rooms, which reflected the progress they had made.[15]

Scott considered all of this some sort of

miracle. "Any economist or accountant would tell us that with our limited unpledged contribution income, plus our in-house generated income from donated items of odds and ends, furniture, et cetera, it is completely impossible to operate a large-scale facility such as ours and provide services such as . . .eleven thousand free meals each month." But with the blessing of God, a lot of work, and contributions of many kinds, "we manage to do it," said Scott. "We make it each and every month and we shall always do so."[16]

Demands on the mission's facilities and resources—not only to help men get off the streets, but especially to serve homeless women and children—were increasing dramatically. The numbers of those in need were swelling. In fact, the need was becoming so great that some board members began offering shelter to homeless women and children in personal rental properties. Determined to address the problem, the mission board began shaping a new ministry aimed specifically at this need.

Accordingly, the mission purchased an old nursing home behind the men's building on Kennedy Street, remodeled it, made it available to women and children, and eventually expanded it into what would become a more permanent family center.

Evanger Conley's story paralleled several at the mission early in the 1980s. Thirty-three years old, from Palestine, Texas, mother of five young children, she had left a failing marriage and come to Fort Worth to live with her sister. In the summer of 1983, when the sister could no longer care for her and her children, Evanger called Union Gospel Mission of Tarrant County. "It was a frightening experience being all alone," she recalled. "I got on the phone and started calling different organizations." Somebody gave her the mission's number.[17]

Evanger and her children were admitted to the women's center family unit, and although she had expected to stay just a few days, by

Evanger Conley.
*Courtesy* Fort Worth Star-Telegram *collection,*
*Special Collections, the University of Texas at*
*Arlington Library, Arlington, Texas.*

November she had become a temporary supervisor over the day-to-day operations of the women's unit. "I originally didn't come here to stay. I came here to get spiritual guidance," she said. "God is my number one thing. . . . It's like the scriptures say: 'The times I'm most afraid I will trust in God,' and that's what I did." Dorothy Harmon, a director of the women's unit, said Evanger had become an invaluable asset to the mission. "She is a very strong, dedicated, and disciplined Christian woman." Not sure how long she would remain at the mission, Evanger hoped ultimately to become an apartment manager and also to do some missionary work. Union Gospel Mission of Tarrant County had given her a place to regroup and rebuild her life.[18]

Evanger knew that she was fortunate to be there, for the mission always had a waiting list and not enough room to accommodate all those in need. In the fall of 1983, in particular, there seemed to be more demand than ever. Dorothy Harmon attributed these growing numbers to a breakdown in the family structure, coupled with the budget cuts of the Ronald Reagan administration. "When I was divorced with three kids, my family helped me over the difficult

times," she said. "Now families aren't able or won't help out." During this period, most single women stayed one week at the mission; women with children often stayed two.[19]

Evanger Conley was one of many preparing to observe Thanksgiving at the mission that November. Bob Scott was planning to serve residents and staff a traditional Thanksgiving Day meal of turkey, cornbread dressing, cranberry sauce, and pumpkin pie. He expected several others to come in off the streets to join them. "We are not publicly announcing we are going to feed everybody who comes here," he said, "although we don't want to turn anyone away. We tried that [feeding everybody] last year and didn't have the facilities to handle it." He was referring to a soup kitchen begun by the mission in 1982. The facilities were overwhelmed. That September alone, more than two thousand people had shown up.[20]

M. J. Neeley had continued to support the mission, not just with fundraising but also with heartfelt encouragement. As 1983 drew to a close, he wrote a letter to the mission, saying, "The real measurement of the good resulting from your dedicated efforts is hidden away in the hearts of the recipients. Although those benefiting can't find the words to express their relief and their appreciation, you know it is in their hearts and you know that God is proud of you for what you have done in His name through 'doing unto others.'" He even claimed, "I am one of the recipients and I am humbly grateful for what the mission's association has given me."[21]

M. J. Neeley was not the only one writing letters to the mission. A number of people sent notes, accompanied by small gifts. "Just wanted to help a little," wrote one. "I'm sorry that I haven't sent more—you deserve it. I've been so busy thinking about myself and my work that I've kind of put you aside." Another gift giver wrote, "My prayers are with you in your caring and reaching people other organizations and

During cold weather, a homeless man wraps himself
in a blanket while waiting for a meal at the mission.
Courtesy *Fort Worth Star-Telegram* collection,
Special Collections, the University of Texas at
Arlington Library, Arlington, Texas.

churches cannot reach. May this little offering be of help." One said simply, "I know you
can use this gift with all the cold weather. With
warm wishes . . . "[22]

A message from Bob Scott early in 1984 provided a good look at the ups and downs of just
one month. The death of H. D. Murray Jr., a
longtime mission supporter, was followed by
a staff member receiving an eye injury from an
accident with a metal grinder. Then came word
of another staff member receiving an "unanticipated sucker punch" from a transient, result-

ing in a concussion and broken left cheekbone.
Next Claude Spence, a resident for many years,
was rushed by ambulance to a hospital with an
illness that would likely keep him convalescing
for a good while. Following all this bad news
came the announcement of upcoming Easter
worship services to celebrate the resurrection
of Jesus Christ and the promise of new life.
Somehow that seemed a fitting conclusion to
the bulletin.[23]

Throughout these trials what sustained
the mission was what had always empowered

The old chapel in the men's building, before remodeling.
Union Gospel Mission of Tarrant County collection.

it—deep faith in the power of Jesus Christ to change lives and an unswerving commitment to care for those he called "the least of these." A clear example of this came in the summer of 1984 when a young woman, alone and weary, walked down the steps leading into the family center. Her name was Deni. She had been traveling on buses for three days from New York. The little bag containing her money had been stolen. In her words, "No one seemed to care." At age twenty-two, she was watching much of her world fall apart. She had been a member of a rock-and-roll band. Abandoned by her boyfriend and flooded out of her apartment, she had quit her job, headed for San Francisco and then to Europe, bouncing from one place to another until returning to New York and then winding up in Fort Worth. One of her only surviving possessions was an electric guitar, which

she carefully guarded. Someone with the Fort Worth Police Department had suggested she go to Union Gospel Mission of Tarrant County.[24]

Descending those steps that day, guitar in hand, she had no idea what to expect but seemed too tired to care. "I was really frightened," she said. "I have never been to a mission before. The only mission I have ever heard of is the Bowery in New York. It has a reputation for winos and drug addicts. The very thought of a mission frightened me. But," she claimed, "this is different. You do care, you *are* Christians. I'm so glad you are here to help me." And help is exactly what she received. Rather than being judged, she was loved, reminded what a precious gift from God her life was, and encouraged about her future and what it might bring.[25]

With help from mission staff, especially

The old chapel, before remodeling.
Union Gospel Mission of Tarrant County collection.

Dorothy Harmon with the family center, Deni soon became ready to step out into the world again, this time with confidence and purpose. She wanted to return to New York—to friends and familiar surroundings—and was encouraged to call her best friend there, who sent her a plane ticket. After farewells to new acquaintances at the mission, she rode with Dorothy Harmon to the Dallas/Fort Worth Airport, excited about beginning anew. "No more running away from my problems for me. Those go with me," she shared, adding, "Thank you so much for your kindness. I will remember this mission and this place for helping me."[26]

That year, 1984, closed as busy as it had begun. During cold nights, chapel benches and the floor had become beds for many left stranded on streets and sidewalks. "But," said Bob Scott, "this is still better than hypothermia. . . .

Railroad boxcars may be sufficient from spring through fall, but they are not very safe during these subfreezing days." The number of people served during the preceding twelve months was also impressive. More than 61,000 beds for men and almost 13,000 for women and children had been provided. In addition, the kitchen staff had served nearly 170,000 meals. Chapel services had also hit high levels of attendance.[27]

Far into the next year, under Bob Scott's leadership, the mission stayed busy. As Christmas 1984 approached, while several of the city's shelters were near capacity, Union Gospel Mission of Tarrant County was totally full. Demand had steadily increased since September. "For about a month now, when we overflow, we've been using our chapel benches," said Scott. "If necessary, we'll put them on carpets on the floor in the building. We've been very busy . . .

but that's okay; that's what we're in business for. We've been operating at about 100 percent capacity. We haven't turned anyone away yet. We won't let them freeze outside, that's for sure." The chapel benches had been used about ten times since November.[28]

The mission's population increased throughout the 1980s. By the spring of 1987, Bob Scott was announcing that construction of an overflow shelter on the second floor of the warehouse building had been completed and passed inspection. Providing space for forty to forty-five beds had become a major project requiring entirely new electrical, water, and gas lines to replace the old, inadequate ones.[29]

On the subject of future expansion, Scott was advising "care and caution." The overflow shelter was helpful but could only be heated, not cooled, making it unsuitable for the summer months. Air conditioning, of course, would entail a significant additional expense. The primary need was more space for women and children at the family center. But that, too, would have to await more funding. One thing he had learned clearly: every time the mission increased its bed capacity, those beds would be quickly filled.[30]

Bob Scott also knew that a number of companies, if given the opportunity, would generously contribute products to Union Gospel Mission of Tarrant County. A good example was Campbell Soup Company. In the summer of 1987, several staff members, in a large Hertz truck, headed to the Campbell plant in Paris, Texas, to load case after case of soup for the mission. Campbell was one of many companies that, unheralded and without fanfare, made tremendously helpful gifts.[31]

That year one thoughtful man took time to describe the lives of many of those helped by the mission. Some might ask why these people didn't simply go out and get jobs. He said it was hard enough to survive until your first paycheck, but even more difficult when you have

hit bottom and have absolutely nothing to start over with. "So what happens?" he asked. "You start trying to survive, not make a living . . . just survive. You start working at labor pools, day labor $3.35 an hour. You work a day and receive a day's pay. Not bad, right? Think again. Eight hours work and you clear about $18.00 after taxes, that is if you show up about 4:30 a.m. to 5:00 a.m. Then be packed in a van with 12 to 20 other people."

Sure, it can be done, he said. After an hour or longer drive, you might arrive at the job site around 8:00 a.m. "If you're lucky, you'll work for someone who doesn't treat you like a bum or trash, work eight to ten hours, then again, if you're lucky, you won't have to wait two or more hours for your ride back to the labor pool to be paid." Upon arrival, "You get paid for the day's work" after a long wait—if, by chance, the labor pool was still open.

"Then it's time to go home," he said. "If you don't get robbed before you get to the bus stop, you're almost there. If the buses have stopped running, then you have to walk to where you call home, a mission, the Salvation Army, or a run-down rooming house . . . then you start the whole thing over again the next day." He did not stop there: "You start saving money, if you don't get robbed, so when you do find a job you can survive to the first paycheck. . . . For a man it's very difficult. For a woman it's almost impossible."

He concluded with some reflections about himself. "I've been down so many times that poverty is a step up. I'm not telling you a sob story. I'm telling you facts about my life and the lives of others who are on the bottom and trying to survive. . . . I'm a survivor," he contended. "Every time I hit bottom I pull myself up by my boot straps and start over again. I'm glad I'm single because a married person would be under unbearable pressure to keep their family fed, clothed, and housed."[32]

By the time he wrote this statement, this man had found a full-time job, was putting some money in the bank, and considering taking night courses at Tarrant County Junior College.

In October 1988, Bob Scott retired as executive director. Letters of appreciation came quickly. "It was a pleasure to work with Mr. Scott," said one writer. "He is a kind and compassionate person; he was a great boss and a good friend. I have much respect and admiration for him." Another said: "Mr. Scott was a patient man with love and admiration towards his fellow man. . . . He tried to take a few acres of land and turn it into a haven for the homeless and street people."[33]

That November Bob was followed as director by V. C. (Chuck) Wiley. A licensed childcare administrator in Texas, he had served as director of an emergency shelter for dependent and neglected children, as well as a juvenile and adult probation officer. Moreover, he had edited small newspapers and been a leader in his church.[34]

One of Chuck Wiley's immediate priorities was to reorganize and strengthen the Bargain Outlet. This program, while needing some attention, was one of the best offered by the mission. Everyone staying at the mission and even those referred by churches or other social service organizations was provided clothing from the outlet at no cost. In addition, people who had suffered losses from floods, fires, and other disasters could receive not only clothing but also furniture and household goods. Mission residents, when ready to leave and live independently, were given the same. Another benefit was the work experience the outlet offered to a number of mission residents—work that not only benefited others but also gave the workers a strong sense of self-worth.[35]

The Bargain Outlet was functioning but needed a major facelift—which is exactly what it got in the first days of 1989. Mike Lopez, a mission supporter, provided the initial guidance as well as much of the physical labor. He was joined by maintenance supervisor Jerry Elliott,

who lent his skills to a number of tasks. Other staff members designed and painted signs. In February, a new position was created—Bargain Outlet operations manager. A well-qualified man, Don Webb, stepped into this leadership role. Don had been food service manager at Diamond Oaks Country Club when he began volunteering one day a week at the mission. The club's ownership changed, putting him out of a job, but that gave him more time to volunteer and made him an obvious choice to run the Bargain Outlet.[36]

At the same time, Chuck Wiley was also working to enlarge and strengthen the New Start program, an intense spiritual program of prayer, counseling, studies, and activities designed to keep the mind and body focused and sober. Its director, Randy Lowe, had been reviewing the applications of more than 130 men who had applied for admission during the preceding three years. In this process he made some noteworthy discoveries. For one thing, most of the successful graduates of New Start spent at least one year, on average, with the program. In his opinion, this relatively long tenure resulted from the fact that most people addicted to drugs or alcohol had not yet taken control of or responsibility for their lives. In his experience, it took a person in this condition three to six months to reach some stability. Only then did real life growth begin. He had also learned that most men entering the program came with only the clothes they were wearing and no job skills. It took time—sometimes a good deal of it—for someone in this condition to work his way back into society. Chuck Wiley, convinced that this was one of the mission's most valuable offerings, made New Start a top priority.[37]

By the winter of 1989, eighteen-year-old Michael Tucker had been at the mission about six months. A San Antonio high school dropout, he had been wandering around town with street gangs. "When I got to Fort Worth, I got a job selling roses on street corners," he said.

"I was just walking by the mission one day, and the cook asked me if I needed a job. I said, 'Yes.' Thanks to everyone here at the mission, I'm gonna get to finish high school, which I wouldn't be able to do on my own."[38]

Don Baker, a mission resident, also had a heartening story to tell. In his early fifties, he had arrived at the mission the previous summer with a broken hip. He was unemployed, and because of his disability, had not been able to find work. "I didn't have any bad feelings about myself," he said. "It was the fact that I was incapacitated at the time, and the people who were hiring wouldn't take me because I couldn't do the work they wanted." Baker started working at the mission in the kitchen, but within a few months had already become office supervisor.[39]

The mission's first role was to offer emergency services—getting people back on their feet with food and shelter. "Then, we want to help folks get back into a mainstream where they can get work. We want to give everyone the help and encouragement they need," said Wiley. Transients were allowed to spend three full nights. Additional time cost $3.50 a night. However, transients could get the fee waived by volunteering to cook, clean, or take on other chores that needed doing. Most so-called staff members began their stays at the mission this way, working at various jobs until proving themselves responsible enough to assume additional duties.[40]

By 1989 Arthur Stukes had been hired as assistant resident manager. Stukes had come from South Carolina to Fort Worth early in the 1980s. Claiming that "this job never has a dull moment," he devoted a lot of time to helping people apply for welfare or Social Security, assisting with transportation needs, and getting supplies for the mission. In his first days on the job, he felt the need to learn what it was like living on the streets and wanted to spend two weeks finding out. He abandoned this learning experience after only four days. "You always feel vulnerable out there. You're always looking behind your back. Nothing is protected," he revealed. "If you turn your head too long, there could be trouble. There are some criminals out there. Don't get me wrong. Not all street people are like that. You find people with a high moral character who are upstanding. They will help you all they can," he said. "But you do have that small, dangerous element out there whose sole purpose is to take from others."[41]

The mission continued to be grounded in evangelistic Christianity, and by this time it was once again asking transients to attend a devotional service before the evening meal. Even so, Chuck Wiley stressed, "We want these people to see that we genuinely care about them. We emphasize the spiritual aspect, but we don't push it. We want to present the Gospel to people, but we don't have anyone choking them and saying they have to accept it."[42]

For those who had accepted Jesus Christ and were seeking to follow in his way, the mission's New Start program was an important lifeline. It was still limited to men, but Wiley hoped to expand the program to include women. Biblical studies and encouraging participants to get involved in churches continued to be the major emphases of the program.[43]

Some impressive numbers were reached by the close of 1989. The mission had provided more than 68,000 beds and 130,704 meals to those in need. It was serving an average of two hundred people every day at a cost of a little more than five dollars per person per day.[44]

But Chuck Wiley's stint as superintendent was about to end. By March of 1990, Frank Van Dyck had succeeded him. These days must have been difficult, especially early in 1991, when Van Dyck described "the people coming to us" as "tense, edgy, and short-tempered." Referring to tension in the Middle East, especially Kuwait, he was convinced that "Jesus's words of 'wars and rumors of wars' in a time when 'the love of most will grow cold' are all too real today

The women's dorm in the women's building.
Union Gospel Mission of Tarrant County collection.

and sobering."[45]

But, as was often true at the mission, large numbers of people were responding to human need. Local television coverage certainly helped. More than two hundred coats were being distributed; turkeys and hams were given, and hundreds of people were clothed. In addition, the New Start program, encouraging Bible study and spiritual growth, was welcoming new members. A quotation on the front page of the mission's newsletter said it well: "Some men look for tall steeples and big bells; Give me a Rescue Mission one yard from Hell."[46]

In the meantime, Don Webb, the mission volunteer who had become operations manager of the Bargain Outlet, was experiencing unanticipated personal challenges in his new role. Although proud of the remodeled four-story facility, having recently been clubhouse manager

of Diamond Oaks Country Club in Haltom City, he was not yet prepared to deal with his new environment. "Talk about culture shock," he said later. "The first six months I worked there, I cried every night. It would tear my heart up to hear an old man tell me how his daughter had abandoned him. It took a while to get my pins under me." After operating the store for a year and a half, in the summer of 1991, Don Webb was selected by the board to replace Frank Van Dyck as superintendent of Union Gospel Mission of Tarrant County.[47]

He walked into a tough situation. Conditions at the mission were almost out of hand. There were "some ugly people," he recalled. "Four guys had taken over and didn't care about what happened to the mission." One day a board member asked one of these men what time, as a so-called staff member, he had come to work.

His answer: "None of your business." The board fired him. Conditions were on the brink of chaos. Don had watched four men steal money and then blame another man, who became so despondent he fled and committed suicide. "These guys had pick handles, iron bars, and mace on their desk," he recalled. "This is how they did business."[48]

The problems were not limited to these men. As the new director, Don asked to speak with the chef. Some dirty man came forward, said he was the chef, and then cooked a horrible dinner—his last. Don fired him. As if this were not bad enough, several men were continuing to run what Don called a "sham chapel service" that in no way reflected the mission's longtime commitment to serve Jesus Christ as lord and savior. So he also fired the chaplain and vowed to begin anew.[49]

Don Webb's goal became clear: to restore the soul of Union Gospel Mission of Tarrant County. He began with the board, lamenting the sad state into which the mission had fallen and reminding members of their responsibilities. The board, determined to make changes, gave him all the authority he requested and also reached out to add new members who could help develop strategies and find resources to move forward.[50]

The mission's board chairman at that time, Tom Redwine, explained the critical importance of Union Gospel Mission of Tarrant County. A former air force officer, Redwine had given much of his recent life to the ministry of the mission. In the fall of 1990, in the 103rd year of the mission, he reminded others that it had been created to meet "severe . . .spiritual and physical needs" and "to alleviate the pain of being hungry and in need, and to bring those persons to Christ." The current goals were much the same, he contended—especially meeting immediate needs of shelter, food, baths, clean clothes, and clean, safe beds.[51]

Redwine clearly spelled out how things worked at the mission during this time. Admissions started after 4:00 p.m. for the men's transient dormitory. Women and children could be admitted at any time to the family center. The men's dormitory was usually full by 7:00 or 8:00 p.m. Chapel services were held Monday through Saturday evenings, as well as Sunday mornings and afternoons. In addition, Bible study in the New Start program held meetings four times a week at 8:00 p.m.[52]

As before, the day began at 5:30 a.m. for transient men. After breakfast at 6:00 a.m., the men who were able reported to various local labor pools or contractors, while those too disabled to work were granted permission to remain inside the mission during the day, and those needing medical help were given transportation to hospitals or clinics. Staffing at this time consisted of a fairly small salaried group, which was far outnumbered by staff members who were receiving their beds and meals in return for their services.[53]

In the Easter season of 1991, a special story was unfolding. The previous fall, a lady named Rosario Mendosa, escaping marital problems, had left Florida in a van with her sister and seven children. The van broke down in Fort Worth near Seminary Drive. Union Gospel Mission of Tarrant County sent a van to rescue the family. The youngest child, an infant whom mission workers named Baby Maria, was in serious condition, unable to cry and almost comatose. Suffering from meningitis, she had to be fed through a feeding tube and wound up in Cook Children's Hospital, where she stayed for months. The mission asked for many prayers on her behalf. Then, one day in February, she began moving her arms and legs—and crying. Declared clear of meningitis, she was able to sit up and no longer in need of a feeding tube.[54]

Her grateful mother was quick to acknowledge God's hand in Baby Maria's recovery—and in her own life. She also began a reconciliation process with her husband. It succeeded to the

The dining room in the men's building, before remodeling.
Union Gospel Mission of Tarrant County collection.

The men's building, before remodeling.
Union Gospel Mission of Tarrant County collection.

point that he came to the mission, and all three of them were soon on their way back to Florida. Rosie checked back several times to let everyone know that things were going well.[55]

As spring brought warmer weather and the men's building population began to drop, the family center was facing just the opposite situation. It was filled to capacity. Day after day the call went out for diapers, toys, and children's clothes. As a result, a much-needed expansion was being planned, which required razing an old vacant rooming house next door. Bids for this job were high, primarily because of the need for asbestos abatement. An inspection by the City of Fort Worth helped solve the problem when the building was declared "residential." This lowered the demolition cost by $5,500 and made the expansion—which would serve increased numbers of women and children—possible.[56]

In the summer of 1991, the *Star-Telegram* carried a front-page story about Union Gospel Mission of Tarrant County that underscored not just one of its biggest challenges, but a major issue confronting many missions and shelters—how to deal with adolescents. Brandy McClain, a fifteen-year-old, had arrived at the mission with her mother and younger sister in the wake of one hardship and disappointment after another. In a poem, she had written ". . . some days I live in a world like HELL." She'd had to grow up fast. "I take care of my sister," she said. "I don't play with dolls. Not that much." She, her thirteen-year-old sister, and a boy named Gainmon Garner, eleven, were the only resident adolescents at the mission's family center. The rest of the twenty-four children were younger than ten.[57]

Brandy had already endured more than her share of tough days. She had been evicted from several homes and run away numerous times—the last episode occurring just before the family's most recent eviction from a dilapidated, rat-infested house with no running water. She landed at the house of a friend whose parents

referred her to an agency operated by Lena Pope Home. From there she wound up back with her sister and mother, living with an aunt who soon put them out on the street.[58]

Brandy was part of a growing nationwide homeless crisis affecting adolescents. Teenagers, especially males, faced a harder time finding shelter, claimed Ann Bowman, the mission's family center director, simply because shelters are more likely to house small children with their parents than teenagers who are on their own. In fact, most shelters would not admit children under eighteen without a parent because of the good chance that they were runaways. Many facilities would not accept children younger than that, even with parents, because of the runaway issue—added to a concern about housing adolescents of both sexes in such close quarters.[59]

So Brandy, with all these bad experiences in her fifteen years, knew that she was fortunate to be living at Union Gospel Mission of Tarrant County. Her life was still difficult—especially at school, where she was two years behind her normal grade. She declared she hated it. But she also had become firmly determined to finish school and get her diploma. A lesson from her father had made an impression. She was stunned when he, trying to get even a dishwashing job, had been turned away because he had not graduated from high school. That, plus watching her mother work hard to earn her high school General Equivalency Diploma (GED), kept her on track to get the job done.[60]

In November of that same year, 1991, a signal, transformational event would occur. Fort Worth businessman M. J. Neeley announced plans to add sixteen studio apartments to the mission, for elderly poor women. Though never joining the board, ninety-four-year-old Neeley had become an avid supporter of the mission and recognized this growing housing need for women. He had learned that in Tarrant County, women sixty-five or older were three times more likely to live alone than a man, with half the chance of being employed and more than twice as likely to be in poverty. "We'd get a few of them in here, and the old ladies would just sit there with a faraway look in their eyes," he observed. "They had given their lives to bringing up two generations, but here in the twilight of their years they were sitting in the best situation they could find."[61]

It was an ambitious, first-of-its-kind project in Tarrant County, what the *Star-Telegram* called "an important precedent for this community." Thanks to the efforts of M. J. Neeley, half of the expected $600,000 cost of the project had already been raised, and hopes were high that the rest would be forthcoming. "I don't know anything like what they are planning," said Maj. Dorothy Rogers, director of the Salvation Army's local retirement home. "It definitely is needed." Don Webb agreed: "We could fill it up tomorrow." In a newsletter article, he shared something of what the mission was about. "Just about all of our folks come to us in the wintertime of their lives. . . . Most of them have little or no means of caring for themselves. They seem to be trapped in a hopelessness of despair," he claimed. "Their days are dismal and gloomy. . . ." The additional housing for older women was aimed at addressing this sad situation.[62]

However, despite the good news about the Neeley project and numerous efforts to bring things under control, one of the saddest episodes in the mission's recent history happened during this period. One morning, over the loudspeaker system, Don Webb heard a deep, impressive voice announcing that the mission's van was preparing to leave and all who wanted to go needed to be on board. Impressed, Don asked; "Who's that making announcements? Send him up here." Within seconds a tall, nice-looking man appeared at his door. "I heard you speak. You have a good voice," he said. "Who are you?" "I am a doctor," he replied. "I was a podiatrist in Dallas, wrote articles for the American Medical Association, gave lectures, drove a Jaguar, had a beautiful wife—all that any man could want—but then got cancer and lost it all." He recounted a tragic tale of losing his wife, his medical practice, and his home. He came to Fort Worth and wound up sleeping in his car. Upon getting hepatitis, he was taken by someone who found him to John Peter Smith Hospital and from there to Union Gospel Mission of Tarrant County. His name was Bernard Bratowsky.[63]

Don Webb, recognizing Bratowsky's abilities, spoke to the board about him and gave him a job as general manager of the downstairs section of the mission. One night Bratowsky and a maintenance man left the mission to drink some beer. As his friend later recalled, they were sitting in a station wagon around 10:00 p.m. on Hudson Street when two men approached the car, and one of them, for reasons unknown, began beating Bratowsky with a baseball bat. He then dragged him out of the station wagon into an alley and took his watch and wallet. His friend, also beaten badly, said that when he regained consciousness, he and Bratowsky walked to a bar and requested help. Bratowsky survived only a few days. All he could tell hospital personnel was that he had been beaten around his head with a baseball bat. John Peter Smith Hospital information revealed that he had listed one brother, an attorney, as a relative. This man came to the mission, surprised and shocked; he had no idea that his brother had sunk to such a pitiful point. Quickly assuming responsibility, he planned and oversaw Bernard's burial at a Catholic cemetery in Dallas.[64]

Violence associated with the mission continued. On the last day of February 1993, one mission worker was killed and another wounded by a resident. The tragedy began when assistant manager Woodrow Jones and maintenance worker Christian Eaker responded to what sounded like gunshots being fired out an open second-story window. They raced upstairs, confronted the resident who somehow had managed to smuggle a gun into the building, and attempted to search both him and his room. A scuffle ensued. The resident pulled a pistol from his pants and shot both men, fatally wounding Eaker. He then calmly walked downstairs and was waiting when police arrived.[65]

Within several months, however, the mission had some much-needed good news to celebrate. Sunday, October 24, marked not only M. J. Neeley's ninety-fifth birthday, but also the official dedication of McFadden Hall, the elderly ladies center in the Otis Lemley building. He had worked diligently to bring this project to fruition. Sixteen new apartments were ready to be occupied. Mission resident Willie Cohran, who had stood beside M. J. Neeley at the project's announcement a year earlier, had long been looking forward to this day. "At least it will be like our little home," she said. "To me, it will seem like I am back home again."[66]

That fall, as Thanksgiving neared, fortunate occupants moved into their new quarters. The weather turned brutally cold. One homeless man who finally found shelter said, "I was numb all over and I wasn't even drinking." Mike Doyle, president of the Tarrant County Homeless Coalition, lamented: "There are so many marginally homeless people—people living with families and friends until their welcome is worn out. Or they're staying in low-budget motels or living in their cars." Union Gospel Mission of Tarrant County took in more than one hundred suffering street people that Thanksgiving, as many as it could possibly handle. A few more stayed outside, refusing to give up their bottles of beer and wine. One mumbled nonsense to passersby. Another, with a puppy he had named Boxcar, sat on the curb saying that he could not get into a shelter because no one accepted pets. For those who made it in from the bitter cold, a full turkey dinner was served.[67]

As December arrived and Christmas neared,

*Star-Telegram* writer Jim Jones reported that the mission had eighty beds in a "back dorm" for street people and "about fifty beds for those who came to the mission and now are part-time staff helping with cooking, cleaning, and other chores." And as usual during this season, Christmas dinner plans were underway. Some three hundred volunteers were preparing to serve a traditional Christmas meal, not in the normal buffet style, but with the homeless guests seated at tables. Volunteers would serve the food in shifts, lead the singing of Christmas carols, and distribute gifts of socks, soap, toothbrushes, candy, and fruit. "We have airline pilots from Grapevine, computer operators, doctors, and attorneys who volunteer," said Don Webb. "They sit down and talk to people. Sometimes it's the first friendly touch from outside that street people have had in months. . . . I wish we could keep that spirit going the other 364 days of the year."[68]

Not only isolated homeless adults, but also an increasing number of children were appearing at the mission's family center. One was twelve-year-old Mary Crain. Her mother had walked out on her husband in Oklahoma and after battling drug and alcohol problems, wound up in Fort Worth. In February 1993, when a fire destroyed their Fort Worth home, Mary and her mother applied for the mission's women-with-children rehabilitation program and arrived with only what they wore and carried.[69]

But what a difference the mission made! By spring of the following year, Mary, who attended a nearby elementary school, was fully involved in its recreational, therapeutic, and educational activities. "Sometimes people know where we live, that we don't have a home like 'most people,'" she said. "When I started going to that school, I was really shy and I hardly knew anybody and it really made me feel bad when they said something about me living at the mission. I'm . . . used to it now. People know me now. I have friends now."[70]

McFadden Hall for Senior Women.
Union Gospel Mission of Tarrant County collection.

Her mother was also making notable progress—learning new skills, holding a good job. Required by the mission's program for "transitionally homeless women" to save seventy-five percent of her income, she had paid off more than $900 in bills, finalized her divorce, and gained invaluable confidence. The next step would be housing placement. She and Mary were now ready to reenter the world. Not all residents could expect to do as well as Mary and her mother, but a surprising number were finding similar opportunities.[71]

These were not the only success stories unfolding during this time. A number of school children who, like Mary's friends, wondered what life was like at Union Gospel Mission of Tarrant County, were getting to see for themselves. On a November afternoon in 1994, several students were greeted by David Conner, mission operations manager, who spoke to them in the chapel and then took them to the cafeteria where some elderly men were eating

dinner. They found the family center full of activity, as a number of children ran out to greet them. One observant visitor remarked, "They all seemed like they were friends, like they were one big family." Another observed, "They have a Coke machine. They have a TV they can watch. And where they eat is like a cafeteria." One summarized what most were probably thinking: "I felt kind of spoiled when I saw what they've got. What you get for one Christmas, they don't get in one whole life."[72]

The man who greeted the students that day, David Conner, had his own remarkable story. He hinted at it to the children in his chapel message, telling them of a privileged childhood wrecked by alcohol and drug addiction and how several months before that day he had wound up at the mission's doorstep in a drunken stupor. There had been, of course, many other events than those he shared that afternoon. In 1981, his wealthy father had left David, then deep into drugs, on the steps of the mission.

David had served two tours in the Vietnam War. He had become a heroin addict. He had also gone through two marriages and spent time in prison.[73]

That first stop at the mission lasted only two or three weeks. Frustrated, he left, and after blowing all his money, reluctantly returned. This leave-and-return routine became a pattern. "Their arms were outstretched every time," he recalled. "If you don't burn all your bridges, it is always there to anchor you." In 1991, David burned those bridges, left the mission, and for the next three years was again on the streets and on drugs. He eventually made his way back and found himself sitting in the chapel listening to a man named Bill Russell preach. Brother Bill's scripture that day spoke directly to David: "I got on my knees, prayed the sinner's prayer, and rededicated my life to Jesus Christ."[74]

The morning he met those schoolchildren, David could honestly say, "I've never been happier. I've found my calling." He still had hills to climb but was well on his way to a new life.[75]

# CHAPTER EIGHT

Don Webb's work through the early to mid-1990s brought some stability and order to the mission. However, it was another man, Don Shisler, who would advance this effort dramatically. He brought with him a fascinating background. A native of Fort Worth, Don had grown up in Haltom City and was a driver for Central Freight Lines. He had become a single parent with two children and an active member of Harvest Baptist Church. One unfortunate event had led to another for Shisler. Attacked by a rare joint disease, he lost his job, underwent hip-replacement surgery, and spent long weeks alone, asking the Lord, "What is next in my life?" At one point he had sought money, believing it would solve his problems. Now, wiser, he asked God, "What am I to do with the rest of my days?"[1]

Sunday after Sunday he sat alone on the back pew of Harvest Baptist Church, pondering that same question. Eventually, after being asked numerous times, he agreed to become a "care group" leader at the church, seeking to serve God but still not sure how. That was about to change, when one Sunday morning Don Webb appeared as a Sunday-school-class guest speaker. He told some of Union Gospel Mission of Tarrant County's story and expressed hope that the class could help with several urgent needs.[2]

Don Shisler responded to this plea and first appeared at the mission as a volunteer. Reporting to Don Webb's office, he wrote letters and ran errands. As he recalled, "God was training me to serve here." By January 1995 he had given outstanding volunteer service for more than a year. When Don Webb announced he was ready to retire, the mission's board voted to name Don Shisler the new executive director.[3]

He could hardly have stepped into a worse situation. "I had never seen anything like it," he said. "The facilities were in shambles. People were stealing whatever they could lay their hands on. There was no accountability." The men's building epitomized these conditions. Wooden panels divided the upper floor into tiny cubicles, with room for only a bed, clothes, and a small lamp. There was no place to sit. Someone described the scene as "a nursing home for men." Occupants included a collection of rough characters who were trying to run the place, living in a haze of cigarette smoke, some sniffing paint, and many riding a circuit that took them from one mission to another and then back again.[4]

The lower level of the men's building, housing about eighty men, resembled an old dormitory. It served two functions: providing some beds for overnight stops and other beds for men who stayed several days. It was common for them to wrap clothing around the legs of the beds to create protected spaces for their few belongings. An indication of how out-of-hand conditions had become was the presence of a six-foot-square wire cage inside the building's Chambers Street entrance. Inside the cage, for protection, was David Conner. The beating of several staff members had made the cage necessary. Through a small opening in its wire, David reached out to welcome men, assign them beds, and collect payment for the night. But he often offered more than that, reaching out to take their hands and to pray with them.[5]

Violence was still all too common in 1995. It took only a small spark—an offhand remark or shove triggered by too much alcohol—to start a fight. When two men tore into each other, David Conner was often the one who intervened. He would remove his glasses, step right in between the men, and tell them to stop, that they were in God's house. More often than not, probably out of sheer surprise, the men stopped fighting. David would then escort them to the office, back them up against opposite walls, facing each other and, as he described it, "Put Jesus Christ in the middle." The rules were clear. Both men were to acknowledge the presence of Jesus and each could speak without being interrupted by the other. "It defused the situation," recalled David. "The power of Jesus Christ is what made the difference."[6]

As the new administrator, Don Shisler knew that things had to change, and that fresh strategies were needed. The first step, with the help of his small staff, was simply to begin cleaning up. The facilities were disheveled and dirty. Someone described the whole place as resembling a flophouse. Slowly it began to take shape, to look organized and cleaner, and at least cared for. Though badly needed, this was only a small, cosmetic step. Serious long-term changes were required, and Don became convinced that a much more involved board of directors was the best way to make those changes happen.[7]

Even the family center needed serious attention. Housed in part of an old nursing home the mission had bought and used with the best of intentions—to help single mothers and their children—the center had become terribly overcrowded. Two, sometimes three families were living in one room. Though shelter and meals were being provided, a healthy environment for mother and children obviously was not.[8]

One particular situation involving a single parent and child was especially troublesome—not a mother but a father and daughter. His name was Frenchy, and he ran the mission kitchen. Frenchy had a criminal history as a forger and safecracker. He had landed at the mission with his young daughter Danielle. Unable to fit into any mission programs, Danielle wound up living in the women's center, staying in one room for a while and then being moved to another. "She was literally being passed around like some unwanted object. It was totally unacceptable," said Shisler. "The most unhealthy, dysfunctional situation you could imagine for a young girl."[9]

One Monday morning, after spending a good while wondering what to do, Shisler came to work and discovered that some residents had created their own solution. Frenchy lived with his fellow kitchen workers on the upper level of the old annex building, which was once the Baptist Rescue Mission. Over the weekend, residents had partitioned off a small piece of it, plus a section of the men's restroom. These newly fashioned quarters could be entered by a door leading to a fire escape. Finally, with this make-do overhaul, Danielle had her own protected place, next to her father, with her own private entrance and restroom. Though curious, Don did not ask and did not want to know where the building materials came from.[10]

An immediate problem had been addressed in a thoughtful, creative way, but a broader, more systematic approach by those responsible for the mission's effectiveness was obviously needed. In many cases, board members attended meetings, listened to reports, made requested decisions, and then left until the next meeting. Shisler, knowing more than this was needed, began phoning board members, visiting with them about their lives, describing some of the deplorable conditions at the mission, inviting them to come take a look, and then to get personally involved. "People are good," he believed. "They just don't know what to do or how to do it. It's a relationship thing." He was convinced that if he and others at the mission took the time necessary to describe the plight of the homeless to those who could make a difference, God would be present and working in that exchange, and they would respond.[11]

He was right. An ever-increasing number of board members began coming regularly, seeing conditions for themselves, and thinking about how to tackle problems. They also saw that the basic, God-centered work of the mission was continuing to change lives. Linda Haywood was one of those whose lives were transformed. Paroled from the Colorado prison system to Fort Worth, she lived with her family for a while but then realized she needed to be out on her own. In the summer of 1995, unable to find a decent place to live, she said: "I asked God where I should go." The answer was Union Gospel Mission, and in July she moved into McFadden Hall. "I had a need to reflect on my life and past, to think about prison where I had just come from. That room was exactly where I was suppose[d] to be at that point and time. Being there allowed me to accept Jesus Christ as my Lord and Savior."[12]

Linda also completed drug classes with Tarrant Community Outreach and was discharged from parole. "Union Gospel Mission allowed me a chance to heal," and it "put me in close contact with our heavenly Father. Whatever accomplishments I made while at the mission, the staff was there to encourage me and help me however they could. I guess you could say that going to Union Gospel Mission was truly a Godsend."[13]

Erwin Fields felt much the same. Plagued for years by drugs and alcohol, having lost his family and everything he owned, Erwin continued his self-destructive ways until, as he said, "One day I was tired, hungry, and broke. I asked a guy if he knew where I could get something to eat. He told me Union Gospel Mission." Erwin

Betty Hedgepeth, a former resident of McFadden Hall and a greeter at chapel services.
Union Gospel Mission of Tarrant County collection.

found the mission and walked in, hoping only to get something to eat. "However, upon arriving, my whole life has changed," he claimed. "Something in my heart was working inside of me. And at that instan[t] I knew without a doubt that the Lord was here . . . And he had been waiting for me."[14]

No matter how much help was needed with mission facilities and programming, desperate, broken people were still being led to new lives. After two months, Fields said the staff had helped him "more than they will ever know. I only hope that one day after I'm gone, I can help someone as the Union Gospel Mission has helped me."[15]

By the end of that year, 1995, Don Shisler had experienced his first Christmas as executive director and could claim that more than $75,000 had been raised during the holiday season. This was good news, but finances were still tight. The $450,000 1995 budget was not likely to be increased the following year, even though the needs of the homeless community likely would be. Don hoped that holiday giving would help the mission meet some long-neglected facility needs, such as replacing the old, outdated electrical heating system in the men's building with gas, and repairing the leaky roof and windows of the Bargain Outlet store that had been damaged in a May hail storm. Across Lancaster from the mission, it was still providing free clothes and furnishings to the homeless and selling any excess to the community. More than $22,000 would have to be raised to meet these needs, but Don was confident.[16]

Meanwhile, Don's plan to get the board more involved and to recruit new members—what he called "a relationship thing"—was continuing to make headway. Board members were visiting the mission and assessing the problems they found there. Even more important, they were enlisting their friends to become board members. Few could have made a bigger impact than Jim Branch when he invited his friend, Cass Edwards, to visit the mission. The Edwards family was one of Fort Worth's first and most prominent. Cass Edwards was a key player in the city's mid-twentieth-century growth and development. In fact, a good portion of Southwest Fort Worth was once the Edwards Ranch.

Cass Edwards liked what he saw. A devout Christian, he was impressed with the mission's God-centered approach and asked if he could join the board. Board members were thrilled but faced an awkward situation when Cass showed up for his first meeting. Because he had not yet been elected, he was asked to wait outside in the hall while a vote was taken. Only then could he enter.

Cass Edwards would become a huge asset to Union Gospel Mission of Tarrant County. Not content to sit on the sidelines, he quickly became involved in its life. He saw the obvious, as-yet-unsolved problems. But more important, he saw potential. He saw what, with good leadership and more resources, the mission

might accomplish. He also knew well the value of Don Shisler's "relationship thing" and acted on it. In much the same way Jim Branch had invited him, Cass encouraged one of his friends, Bob Crow, to visit the mission and join its board.

Bob Crow was no ordinary Fort Worth citizen. Executive vice-president of First National Bank until 1982 when he retired to become executive director of the Amon G. Carter Foundation, he had advised and worked with Fort Worth's most prominent citizens and business leaders. He served on numerous boards and councils and was one of Fort Worth's most prominent, respected leaders.[17]

In 1996, when Bob Crow retired from the Carter Foundation, Cass Edwards, knowing that Bob would be besieged with numerous offers to help various causes, called him immediately and invited him to come learn about the mission. "He stayed with it," remembered Bob. "He told me, 'the Lord needs you at the Union Gospel Mission.' I could not refuse that." He soon became a new board member.[18]

Bob Crow quickly realized how much needed to be done for the mission to reach its potential. Operating on a hand-to-mouth basis, it was perceived as "a street church," he said, not "a service agency." One facility breakdown followed another. At his first board meeting, a major concern was how to remodel the bathroom in the old nursing-home building. The estimated cost was $40,000. Cheap items had been bought and then installed by residents. In his opinion, the mission simply had to be a better steward, to plan for "the long haul" and have money for ongoing programs.

To meet immediate needs, Don Shishler's "relationship thing" would again prove invaluable. Nancy Snyder, daughter of prominent Fort Worth citizen Rice Tilley, appreciated the fact that her father had been instrumental in helping the mission build its new facilities in 1979. Becoming increasingly involved in helping the mission meet emergency needs, she invited friend Kay Fortson to take a tour with her, and pointed out, in particular, the need to remodel bathrooms. Kay asked how much the bathroom project would cost. The next day Don Shisler had a $40,000 check in hand.[19]

During this period perhaps nothing so dramatically portrayed the plight of the homeless as a lengthy local newspaper article in the summer of 1997. In order to experience and relate to others what it is like "to live on the streets," Jeff Guinn, writer for the *Star-Telegram*, decided to spend a week doing just that. Union Gospel Mission of Tarrant County would become part of the story.[20]

Wearing old, torn clothes, Guinn began his experience on a Monday morning at the Greyhound bus station in downtown Fort Worth. Leaning against a wall, he said "Morning" to several people passing by, getting no response, not even a glance—his first taste of feeling invisible. After eating a sack lunch at the First United Methodist Church Mission, he began a long walk north, crossing the Trinity River bridge, making his way up North Main Street, growing tired and hungry. With darkness approaching and finding no evening meal, he scouted out some closed businesses looking for a safe, hidden place to sleep. Finally, finding an unlocked delivery van, he climbed inside, moved a dolly to create some room, and stretched out for the night. By 4:00 a.m., cold and unable to sleep, he ate a can of Vienna sausages saved from yesterday's lunch and walked five miles to East Hattie Street. Here, situated among crack houses, prostitutes working street corners, and drug addicts desperate for the next fix, was a program called Loaves and Fishes that offered lunch to the homeless. Guinn was led to the building's basement, where some two dozen men and women sat at battered tables waiting for food. When several plastic baskets containing cold, soggy sandwiches appeared, everyone began grabbing. Guinn had no complaints. He

was glad to have something to eat.[21]

He had already decided that Union Gospel Mission of Tarrant County would be his next stop. What he did not know was how frightening that walk would be. He planned to head down East Vickery Boulevard to Tennessee Street and follow it to East Lancaster, which would lead him to the mission. "The stench of decaying garbage was overpowering," he recalled. "My eyes stung from sweat dripping in them. The remnants of cold chili dogs boiled in my stomach." After covering a few blocks, he realized someone was following him. The man caught up with him, grabbed his shoulder and said, "Gimme money." Guinn kept moving and when grabbed again, knocked the man's hand away and walked faster. Reaching Tennessee Street, he heard the man coming up behind him and thought a fight was imminent. However, suddenly and surprisingly, the man turned around and went the other direction.[22]

Guinn then saw why. Ahead of him were three men standing silently facing him. Quickly trying to decide whether to turn around or approach them, he chose the latter, looked straight ahead, and walked past them. They never moved or spoke. Finally reaching the mission around 2:00 p.m., he saw several men sitting on the sidewalk waiting until 6:00 when they could come in for the night. Several other men and women were lying in the shade across the street. Around 4:00, Guinn told a staff member that he would like to have some "day work." He was quickly brought inside and introduced to a large, bearded man called Big Jerry, someone he described as "straight out of a Dickens novel."[23]

Informed he would be working an 11:00 p.m. to 7:00 a.m. shift and cleaning a coliseum, Guinn attended a required chapel service led by a Southwestern Baptist Theological Seminary student, and then joined fellow workers for an early five o'clock supper.

He noticed that the recent arrivals quickly divided into racial groups. His observation:

"The blacks hated the whites; the whites hated the blacks. The Hispanics hated everyone and everyone hated them." Because he had tried to visit with some Hispanics, the white clique would have nothing to do with him. Staff members told him that these racial boundaries and attitudes were typical.[24]

Regardless, he had work to do and a long night ahead. Around 10:00 p.m. Big Jerry gave instructions, distributed sack lunches, and announced that checks would be issued in about a week. He then broke the news: "You're cleaning out the Will Rogers Coliseum." This was not good news. Guinn, having attended many events there, knew well the size of that building and never imagined that one night he would be cleaning it. He and his work partners were then driven in an old Lincoln Town Car to the coliseum to be met by city employee G. W. Mattingly, who divided them into work groups. One would break down and store tables and chairs; another would pick up trash from the day's cutting horse show. Mattingly addressed every worker as "Mister" because, as he told Guinn during a break, he respected homeless workers, admitting that during "a bad spell" he, too, had slept under some bridges.[25]

The night was filled with hard work—mopping floors, cleaning bathrooms, polishing railings. Three of the guys who had been in prison together talked about friends still there. At 3:30 in the morning, Mattingly declared a one-hour meal break. Guinn noticed that most of the men used five minutes of that hour to eat and the remaining fifty-five to sleep. At 4:30, work resumed as the men were led to the John Justin Arena and Will Rogers Auditorium, where they continued sweeping and mopping until Guinn's hands were blistered. Then around 7:00 a.m. Mattingly thanked the workers, filled out forms to be delivered to Big Jerry, and took everyone back to the mission.[26]

For Jeff Guinn, a long new day was just beginning. While his fellow sweepers and mop-pers ate a late breakfast at the mission, he used the time to take a soapless shower with some watery shampoo someone found. He used a sheet for a towel and then headed out to the street to face the day. "Walking back downtown, I felt exhausted. It was hard to put one foot in front of the other," he said. "My stomach growled and I felt I'd been frivolous to choose cleanliness over food. Woozy, I slumped on a bench at West Fourth and Houston Street. For the first time, I sensed people were looking at me, but only because I clearly was in no shape to approach them for a handout."[27]

Guinn would have more eye-opening experiences in the days ahead, but already had dealt with more than he could have predicted. What dominates his account and seems to overshadow all else is how frightening it is to be alone on the streets—always looking over your shoulder, wondering where to find some food and, after dark, trying to locate a safe place to sleep. Union Gospel Mission of Tarrant County gave him a chance to work, paid him, and treated him with respect. He acknowledged and remembered that.[28]

Guinn's account attracted widespread attention, focusing light on people and conditions that, for the most part, had remained in the shadows unnoticed or ignored. One concrete, tangible result would materialize a year later with the creation of the Fort Worth Day Resource Center for the Homeless. This kind of place had been long needed. Its purpose was to serve the homeless by providing daytime refuge from the weather, plus a reading room, laundry facilities, and restrooms. Another result of this powerful piece was the expansion of transitional and permanent supportive housing programs across Tarrant County.[29]

Meanwhile, in the fall of 1997, human needs were pressing hard at the mission's door. There was a critical need to help single mothers with children. Until recently, the family center had been able to admit about three families a week.

But now it was at its fifteen-family capacity and turning away eight or more families every week. "Not long ago we would have a few come by," said Don Shishler, "but nothing like we're experiencing now." Christmas that year revealed even more pressing needs. "Too many people showed up," he recalled. "We had volunteers helping, and David Conner and I dealt with things the best we could, but we were flooded with people needing food and shelter. I got really tired. Even my voice was gone."[30]

It was glaringly apparent that something more than reaction to one crisis after another was needed. Once again Don Shisler's "relationship thing" would prove dramatically effective. Cass Edwards had recruited Bob Crow to join the cause. Now he and Bob planned to enlist another key person. Larry Eason, having founded and long directed Fort Worth's Child Study Center, had recently retired and was establishing a consulting business. On a mid-summer day in 1998, Bob and Cass met with Larry, explained the importance of their cause, why they were involved, and then asked him to make Union Gospel Mission of Tarrant County his first consulting client. What they needed was a mission master plan, an agreed-upon, comprehensive game plan outlining a step-by-step process to move into the future. The mission, they contended, simply had to progress beyond responding to a myriad of immediate needs without some larger strategy that could guide and sustain it in the years ahead.[31]

Larry Eason was the perfect choice for this assignment. An affable, positive, talented person, he had gained valuable experience in planning, recruiting qualified people, working with boards of directors, and turning good intentions into reality. He could not refuse Bob Crow and Cass Edwards's request. How could he? Here were two of the city's most respected citizens asking him to join them in a project helping "the least of these," to which they were deeply committed. He agreed, was hired by the mission on a monthly basis, and was soon hard at work.[32]

Larry could hardly believe conditions at the mission. "The facilities were absolutely horrible," he recalled. In addition to the men's building, the old nursing home, and McFadden Hall, there were two rundown, three-story brick buildings. One was used for laundry and various services; the other apparently housed some homeless men. "They were dilapidated," said Larry. "They looked like old brick buildings that had been here forever." In addition, an old triple-wide trailer resting on concrete blocks sat right in the middle of things. Bell Helicopter had donated it. Mission directors, thinking it might be used for offices, had spent $30,000 to upgrade it. And, as if this were not unsightly enough, in one corner of the parking lot stood a large billboard whose base obstructed the flow of cars and people. "There was no future in this," he said. "It [upgrading the trailer] was throwing good money after bad, and the board knew it. They just did not know what to do."[33]

By the end of September Larry was ready to come to the board with a list of questions. For example: What are the mandates of Union Gospel Mission of Tarrant County? That is, what must be done according to its charter and regulations? What are the strengths of UGM-TC? What are its weaknesses? What are the opportunities of the mission? What are its threats? And what are the critical issues the mission could expect to face over the next five years?[34]

Answers to these questions would shape the plan to lead the mission into many tomorrows. The top responses to these mandates were to feed and clothe the hungry, preach the gospel, and house the poor. The major strengths were listed as the staff, the loyal donors, and particularly that the mission was Christian based. However, the staff also led its list of weaknesses—not its quality, but its small size. Lack of trained volunteers, security, and funding followed closely behind. Viewed as mission opportunities were

The old Cox Sheet Metal building.
Union Gospel Mission of Tarrant County collection.

An Easter sunrise service near the old Cox Sheet Metal building.
Union Gospel Mission of Tarrant County collection.

collaboration with the Presbyterian Night Shelter and the Salvation Army, as well as educating the community about the plight of the homeless, public service announcements, and erecting a historical marker. Also ranked high was a "service and work" program for the homeless.[35]

Out of this process, within a few months, came Union Gospel Mission of Tarrant County's first comprehensive strategic plan. Program targets included collaborating with numerous organizations helping the homeless, expanding services to women with children, working with others to provide high-quality childcare, and expanding involvement with churches in the community. Some of the most dramatic goals targeted facilities. The old Cox Building, used for maintenance and storage, and the annex building would both be demolished, and where those had stood a new family center—the John and Jo Catherine Cox Building—would be constructed. It would be a two-story facility containing a chapel, kitchen and cafeteria, laundry facilities, offices, childcare space, and a library and tutoring area for children. In addition, the men's building would be remodeled, and the old family center, once vacated, would be converted to expand service to women without children.[36]

Operational and security issues were also addressed, but one of the most important, far-reaching subjects was funding. The strategic plan called for a feasibility study to determine if the mission could raise the money necessary to sustain and build the programs and facilities outlined. The plan called for a $4,000,000-plus capital campaign to fund the described projects. The money would be used for capital needs, an endowment for capital purposes, and start-up funds for new services. It would also expand Bargain Outlet operations to provide additional resources for the various ministries of the mission. Immediately following the capital campaign, the plan called for an annual plan for year-round fundraising.[37]

In March 1999 campaign developments began moving quickly. The mission board approved hiring Cargill Associates in Fort Worth to direct the effort. That same month, Larry Eason distributed a draft strategic plan for board adoption, and director Bob Crow announced that the mission would be receiving approximately $1,400,000 from the Cox estate. Fort Worth resident John Cox had been a trustee of the Mabee Foundation. Upon his and his wife JoAnne's deaths, their wills stipulated that the bulk of their estate was to be divided among four charities, including Union Gospel Mission of Tarrant County. By October, architects Tod Hanson and Gerald Schwarz were retained as architects for the new family center. The following month Cargill Associates called the campaign goals "attainable" and recommended the campaign be named "New Beginnings."[38]

In the winter of 1999, encouraged by this longer-range, comprehensive approach and reassured that major new steps were possible, board members authorized a $6.5 million capital campaign—by far the most ambitious in the mission's long history. The project began quietly, with board members and representatives of the mission privately lobbying individuals and foundations. The case was not hard to make. The mission was serving more than three hundred residents and guests per day. Though men were still a majority, the number of women and children had doubled in just five years. Only five rooms were available for this increasing population, sometimes requiring three families to be crowded into each one. In addition, the men's building, with eighty beds, stayed so full that late arrivals were forced to sleep on chapel pews. When these were filled, the only space remaining was the chapel floor. The needs could not have been clearer. By this time Larry Eason had become so enthusiastic about the ministry and future of Union Gospel Mission of Tarrant County that he resigned as consultant and asked to become a member of the board. On

December 16, he was elected.[39]

No time was wasted addressing these problems. In January, stepping up immediately as a board member, Eason recommended demolishing two old mission buildings and removing the triple-wide trailer from the property. A few weeks later, architects presented drawings of the new family center—estimated cost, $4,000,000. By mid-June the old buildings scheduled for demolition, as well as the trailer, were gone, and the board committed $1,000,000 of the Cox estate to the campaign.[40]

During the following months, fundraising continued quietly, but intensely and successfully. By the end of January 2001, the campaign went public with an announcement that $4,200,000 in pledges had been committed, including a $500,000 challenge grant from the Mabee Foundation. However, the estimated cost of the new family center soon swelled to $5,000,000, increasing the overall cost to be covered by the campaign. In light of these estimates, the board decided to divide the campaign into two phases. Phase I would focus on

Demolition of Cox Sheet Metal Building.
Union Gospel Mission of Tarrant County collection.

the family center. Phase II, to begin later, would raise funds to renovate the men's building.[41]

That spring the board invited five construction firms to bid on the new facility and announced a September 13 groundbreaking. These plans, though designed for local needs, were addressing a problem that reached far beyond Fort Worth. In November 2001, the Urban Institute of Washington, DC, published a report saying that, nationwide, homelessness was increasing rapidly, and that on any given day at least 800,000 people were homeless. Alarmingly, that number included some 200,000 children in homeless families. The report called this situation a "revolving-door" crisis, claiming that although many people left the homeless category quickly, far more were entering it every day. The numbers were large and alarming. The report estimated that as many as 10 percent of all poor people in the nation were homeless at one time or another during a twelve-month period, and called for a concerted national strategy to address the problem—one that included new housing opportunities and community building programs. Its message was clear: "Only strategies that address systemic problems as well as provide emergency relief can eliminate homelessness in this country."[42]

In the days ahead, as the mission staff worked with issues related to moving into the new family center and developing some new programs, the board turned its attention to two major concerns, one of which was term limits for members. This was a tough issue but one that needed to be addressed. With no term limits, some directors had served for more than twenty years, leaving little opportunity for the board to elect new members. Vacancies occurred only with retirements and deaths. Larry Eason, elected board chairman in March 2003, made changing this situation a priority. By the next month, at their April meeting, directors were discussing not only rotating terms but also what size the board should be. These

The John and Jo Catherine Cox building.
Union Gospel Mission of Tarrant County collection.

discussions continued until September, when members voted to amend the mission's bylaws to create a rotating board of directors. Each member would serve a three-year term. Although several longtime members were given life terms, the way was finally opened to elect new members every year.[43]

The other important issue that drew ongoing attention and action was fundraising. A direct-mail approach had been suggested as a way to increase donations dramatically. With this in mind, the board agreed to interview several direct-mail firms and in July 2003, after having heard a number of presentations, retained Douglas Shaw & Associates of Chicago to launch this effort. Shaw had proposed using no stock photos or stories and tailoring the mailings

specifically to Union Gospel Mission of Tarrant County. The board liked this approach and authorized $103,000 to get started. The prediction—and hope—was that the mission would net $4,754 after costs and gain 4,174 new donors with the initial effort. But the campaign far exceeded expectations. By December, the mailing had raised $107,698 and enlisted a record number of new donors. That month's mailing focused on Christmas, announcing that the mission was serving more than seven hundred hungry people, providing them with warm clothing, coats, and blankets, and giving every child a new toy on Christmas Day. It claimed that a ten-dollar gift would feed three people, twenty dollars would feed six, and fifty dollars could provide food for fifteen people. In addition, it featured a photo of children who had designed holiday cards that could be bought for fifteen dollars a pack.[44]

On Christmas morning that year, Rolf Larson was preparing for the role he had played the last eight years—Santa Claus. Discovering that the mission had no Santa Claus, he volunteered, and began what became an annual tradition, handing out toys to the mission's homeless children. "Every year this costume company has a complimentary Santa suit all laid out for me," he said. "I don't even have to call them anymore. And every year the suit keeps getting better." This Christmas Day he had started early, around 7:15 a.m., and was joined by Mrs. Claus—his wife, Gay—who said, "This is the most fun thing we do all year."[45]

Christmastime at Union Gospel Mission of Tarrant County had become a major event. "We had something going on every day during the Christmas holidays," said Don Shisler. "It's the busiest day of the year for us, but it can be a sad time for the homeless. They are displaced and separated from their families and friends. It is during this time that the community helps us with gifts that our people need just to survive."[46]

Rolf and Gay Larson were joined by many volunteers whose impact would last far beyond Christmas. Shisler claimed that the larger pool of holiday volunteers, many of whom he never met, helped keep the mission afloat all year. People who called in at Christmas could sometimes be persuaded to serve at other times during the year. "The mission tries not to lose those call-in volunteers, because they are needed continuously, and their help is worth about fifteen dollars an hour." By this time the mission was logging more than 1,700 volunteer hours every month.[47]

Few could have imagined how full and exciting the next year would be. In March of 2004, the board turned its attention to the men's building and began lengthy discussions about how to fund its remodeling, as well as how to handle the large displacement of residents the project would create. It was no small problem. Substantial additional space would have to be found to house the men for however long the construction lasted. A solution came with word that the nearby Pepsi Building was for sale. A plan was soon formulated. The mission could buy the Pepsi Building directly down the street, transform it into a warehouse, and then reconfigure it.[48]

The plan, though large and costly, moved forward. The Pepsi Building was purchased and converted into a warehouse. In the meantime, the mission board enlisted architect Tod Hanson to produce drawings showing how another building, the old Ofco warehouse, could be remodeled to create temporary rooms for men while the new men's building was under construction. By that fall, the cost estimate for the work on the men's building was released—$2,600,000—and the board authorized a $3,000,000 capital campaign. While all this was happening, the mission's direct-mail effort was proving so successful that board members voted not only to repeat it but also to double its size.[49]

An increasing number of churches wanted to volunteer at the mission. Bylaws charged the board's Mission Partners/Church Relations Committee with developing standards and criteria to determine which churches would be considered mission partners. Some churches that had expressed interest in volunteering were being called "not really Christian in nature." To deal with this situation, the committee met and chose to make the doctrinal statement of the Association of Gospel Rescue Missions the core of its criteria recommendations. Acceptance of six statements was fundamental:

• We believe the Bible to be the inspired, infallible, ultimately authoritative Word of God.
• We believe there is one God, eternally

existing as Father, Son, and Holy Spirit.

• We believe that the Lord Jesus Christ is deity, that He was born of a virgin, that we are redeemed by his atoning death through His shed blood, that He bodily resurrected and ascended into Heaven, and that He will come again in power and great glory.

• We believe that men are saved through a direct, personal encounter with the risen Lord, at which time they are regenerated by the Holy Spirit. This event we hold to be an experience, rather than a doctrinal supposition.

• We believe in the present ministry of the Holy Spirit, by whom Christ indwells each believer enabling him to live a godly life of obedience as he reaches for maturity.

• We believe the Holy Spirit unites all true believers in the Lord Jesus Christ and that together they form one body, the church.

The board accepted this recommenda-tion and then moved forward to strengthen the partner church program.

In March, while issues including every-thing from partner churches to construction were being decided, something much more vis-ible and eye-catching was happening. Neigh-borhood leaders were in the process of turning a vacant lot off East Lancaster into a park for the homeless. And to help make it attractive, a local artist, Jo Dufo, recruited volunteers and sup-plied paint to create a large mural on the side of the building facing the park. She oversaw the project and enlisted mission residents to help paint. "We want to beautify the community, up-lift it," said Flora Brewer, president of the Near East Side Neighborhood Association. "Just because there are homeless shelters here, it doesn't mean that's all that can happen there." Some 150 neighbors, volunteers, and residents joined to paint this large mural with bright im-ages of earth, children, cowboys, and animals. "This is something the homeless can view to

The remodeled men's building.
Union Gospel Mission of Tarrant County collection.

give them hope," said Don Shisler. The place it overlooked would be named Unity, and it still serves its much-needed purpose today.[50]

By the time 2004 drew to a close, Union Gospel Mission of Tarrant County had taken historic steps and made amazing progress. The board had authorized a $3,000,000 campaign to renovate the men's building. The mission was reaching out to more than three hundred residents and guests each day. That year it had served some 141,200 hot meals and 29,290 sack lunches to hungry men, women, and children. The men's shelter was housing almost two hundred every night. The women's shelter now offered thirty-two beds; the new family center had twenty-six rooms for mothers and children; and McFadden Hall was providing sixteen rooms for older women.[51]

The statistics were telling a big story. In 2004, more than 56,100 nights of safe shelter were given to homeless men as well as 40,770 nights of safety to women and children. In addition, through the mission's thrift store and daily distributions, more than 1,100 people received clothing and household items.[52]

One of the most important developments was the expanding use of community organizations. For instance, the Tarrant Council on Alcohol and Drug Abuse was sending caseworkers to provide assessments and referrals for those in need. In 2004 alone, 146 people had been involved in substance abuse recovery programs. Also, with mental illness so prevalent among the homeless, the mission had recruited Mental Health Mental Retardation (MHMR) of Tarrant County, which screened and assisted 128 people with mental health-related needs and provided emotional help to many. That was not all. In the fall, the University of Texas at Arlington, having partnered with the mission, provided residents with 950 hours of counseling services.[53]

By now, an impressive number of agencies and institutions were helping dramatically with educational and vocational training. The Fort Worth Day Resource Center for the Homeless, across the street from the mission, and the Workforce Center of the Texas Temporary Assistance to Needy Families (TANF) were providing job training and placement assistance to residents. In addition, the University of Texas at Arlington's School of Social Work was offering computer literacy classes, and the YWCA was providing childcare for young children. At the same time, the Parenting Center was giving the mission's children a much-needed sense of security. Added to all this was the Sunshine Club and Campfire Boys and Girls programs offering role models and lots of fun to more than 230 children each year.[54]

Every one of these promising programs was undergirded by spiritual principles and programming. Chapel services were being held daily. Ministers from local church communities gave freely of their time, again and again delivering encouraging Bible-centered messages to residents as well as to those who wandered in off the street. Volunteers were also critically important. During the previous year, they had given more than 22,000 hours.[55]

Contributions may have supplied the most revealing numbers, however. Almost 39 percent of donations were coming from foundations, while gifts from individual donors comprised more than 52 percent of the mission's budget. Almost 4 percent came from churches, 5 percent from businesses, and a smaller percentage from community organizations. The financial numbers for 2004 were more than impressive. Annual operating contributions for 2002 were $655,676 and for 2003, $626,471. But 2004 was a record. Contributions that year totaled $1,444,793. Union Gospel Mission of Tarrant County was moving forward in unprecedented ways.[56]

The mission's fundraising efforts were in high gear in the following months. Mass-mailing results had been so positive that in April of 2005, the board voted to spend $377,775 for a

Ron and Deborah Hall serving dinner to residents and guests.
Union Gospel Mission of Tarrant County collection.

1,005,000-piece mailing with the expectation of identifying 10,868 new donors. And Phase II of the New Beginnings Campaign was well underway, with a $3,000,000 goal to completely remodel and expand the men's building, create a new learning center in the new Cox Building, purchase additional property adjacent to the mission, and expand the parking lot. With funds remaining from the initial campaign, plus an estate gift, this effort had begun with more than $500,000. By the fall of 2005, board members and their families had pledged an additional $600,000, raising hopes that the campaign could be completed within a few months.[57]

As important as these financial gains were, even more important were lives being changed. Here the mission's spiritual foundation figured large. A man named Tom was a prime example. Tom had been hit hard by one loss after another. After losing both parents, he went through two marriages, and becoming engaged a third

time, lost his fiancée in a car accident. Drinking was his response to the hurt and depression. He bounced from one recovery program to the next but, somehow, was still able to hold a job as a McDonald's manager until quitting in 2003 and sinking into depression and alcohol abuse. "I couldn't accept the fact that God could forgive me," he said.[58]

Having lost his home and living out of his car, Tom finally came to the mission for help. But even that step did not begin well. Repeatedly, he would leave the mission to drink and was kicked out three times. Each time he returned, determined to try again. To his surprise, he was always let back in. The last time he returned, a staff member had a long talk with him about forgiveness. "That day it finally hit me," said Tom. "From that day forward, I've had to pray, 'Lord, help me with this.' And he has." Following that fateful evening, Tom remained sober, saying that God's grace penetrated his heart

Ron and Deborah Hall with their son, Carson.
Union Gospel Mission of Tarrant County collection.

and that he finally understood Christ's words about forgiveness.[59]

Tom went from life's depths to helping run the mission's warehouse, distributing clothes to the homeless. How he found a new life was expressed eloquently in his own words:

> There's a community of people walking and trying to walk with the Lord. They'll go out of their way to help. They won't blow you off. And they share the Word. It all boils down to the Lord. Give yourself a break and let God do it. Trust him to help you do anything and everything. The Cross finished it once and for all."[60]

In the meantime, juggling construction projects occupied much of the mission's next months. In September 2006, board members chose to exercise the mission's option to purchase the Pepsi-Cola warehouse from Paulos Properties for $325,000. The mission would pay for all repairs and use the building for storage.[61]

At the same time, something else was happening that would have a large, unforeseen impact on Union Gospel Mission of Tarrant County. It was a book. Ron Hall, an upscale art dealer, had been drawn to the mission by his wife, Deborah, an enthusiastic volunteer. There he met a homeless black man named Denver Moore. Over a period of time their very different lives became closely intertwined—a relationship that resulted in a book entitled *Same Kind of Different As Me*, written by both men, each in his own style.[62]

Few could have predicted the book's success. Popular far beyond the local market, it wound up on the *New York Times* bestseller list. Ron Hall and Denver Moore were in big demand, speaking before large audiences, describing their unlikely friendship and, whether intending to or not, bringing widespread publicity to Union Gospel Mission of Tarrant County. Denver became especially well known, so much so that several of his frequent sayings were being called "Denver-isms." Some examples: "Most people have eyesight, not insight." "We is all homeless just workin' our way home." "Most folks think they the only customer God has." And "There's too much Bible study'n and not enough Bible doin'."

The book's influence was powerful, and it affected fundraising. Mission income was boosted dramatically as donations came in from around the nation. Even movie rights were soon being seriously discussed. With more than one million copies sold, *Same Kind of Different As Me* would not only give Union Gospel Mission of Tarrant County national attention but, even more important, increase public awareness of the many desperate, barely surviving Americans who did not know where their next meal or bed might be.[63]

The book came at a propitious time. As the mission was striving to expand and to improve its services, growing national attention was being focused on homelessness. The National Alliance to End Homelessness published a report contending that in the decade following World War II, widespread homelessness did not exist, primarily because of a strong housing market and a system of public support that reached most people in need. Beginning in the 1960s, however, the situation changed. Much affordable rental housing became converted to higher-priced housing while, at the same time, many hospitals for the mentally ill were closing in response to growing support for community-based housing and care. This was not all bad, but did lead to a scarcity of affordable rental housing. The report reflected what was already becoming obvious: there were 5.2 million more low-income households needing housing than there were available, affordable units. And making matters worse, communities were not creating enough housing and services for the mentally ill to keep pace with the institutions being closed.[64]

Perhaps even more revealing and troubling was the report's focus on what it termed "chronic homelessness." This was defined as long-term repeated homelessness. The description would have been familiar to most of the staff at Union Gospel Mission of Tarrant County: "Virtually all chronically homeless people have a disability. Many . . . have a serious mental illness like schizophrenia, alcohol or drug addiction, and/or chronic physical illness. Most chronically homeless individuals have been in treatment programs, sometimes on dozens of occasions." It complemented the federal government's definition, which went further: "Homelessness means sleeping on the streets or in a place not meant for human habitation or sleeping in an emergency shelter." While the chronically homeless did not represent a majority of the homeless population at any point in time, they consumed a disproportionate share of shelter use.[65]

These were not just bureaucratic categories to the people running Union Gospel Mission of Tarrant County. They were real people finding refuge and sleeping wherever they could. They were under bridges, in dark alleys, in parks, and on sidewalks. With all their possessions in backpacks and plastic bags, they were standing in long lines at shelters on East Lancaster, hoping for a meal and, even more, for a bed. Their numbers were growing, and while some citizens managed never to see them, others were becoming increasingly concerned and searching for ways to address this inexcusable situation in a flourishing city.[66]

The *Star-Telegram* had made the problem hard to ignore with a front-page article entitled "The Hidden Homeless": "The forgotten are always on display along East Lancaster Avenue. Homeless people fill the sidewalks looking for food, work, drugs, or a spot in one of the shelters," the story began.

But look deeper into the surrounding overgrown landscape. A hidden world emerges. Follow a steep, rocky path down a hill into a thicket of trees near Interstate 30, just east of downtown. Push aside the branches; step over strewn garbage. Find a clearing where tents are pitched around a fire pit. A hand-painted sign on one tent reads: "DO NOT ENTER UNLESS ENVITED. KNOCK FIRST THIS IS MY HOME."[67]

This was the "home" of fifty-seven-year-old Toevarieshka Voncruchien, known as Toevar. Tattooed, wiry, wearing Dickies overalls, Toevar was one of hundreds of local people living outdoors in tents, shanties, and lean-tos. Although Toevar regularly walked to nearby Union Gospel Mission of Tarrant County for lunch, many of these homeless vagabonds avoided shelters, preferring their precarious lives to crowds and rules. Some women and even families were among their number, but most were single men. Mental illness and substance abuse were common. Crime was rampant. Many of these struggling homeless were hidden among trees near major roadways or the Trinity River in Fort Worth. Some were camped in the woods of northeast Arlington.[68]

Information about Toevar and others in similar circumstances was the result not only of good newspaper reporting, but also of renewed community efforts to understand and address this problem. The Tarrant County Homeless Coalition, utilizing volunteers, was doing its best to locate and venture into camps to get a comprehensive count and survey of the county's homeless population. The coalition estimated that in the previous ten years the population had doubled, to more than five thousand. In addition to this initiative, Fort Worth's homeless coordinator, Otis Thornton, was giving Mayor Mike Moncrief and two city councilwomen an eye-opening tour of the homeless in their city. The mayor, looking for ways to address the problem and contending it was reaching a critical mass, admitted, "We need a game plan." After visiting several shelters and numerous campsites near major thoroughfares, the group arrived at Toevar's tent. Understandably surprised, he shook Moncrief's outstretched hand. When the mayor introduced himself and asked, "What services can the city provide to make your life better?" Toevar shrugged and responded, "Just leave me alone, I guess." The mayor chuckled, "At least you're honest."[69]

By this time, more than two hundred cities across the nation had made commitments to end chronic homelessness and had launched ten-year plans. Fort Worth was the largest city in the nation not included in this number, but that was about to change. Moncrief, ready to act, appointed a Mayor's Advisory Commission on Homelessness with Don Shisler and Larry Eason as members. For months, the commission pored through reports, listened to testimony, and discussed recommendations. When the

report was released in the summer of 2008, its title reflected Jeff Guinn's 1997 "No Direction Home" *Star-Telegram* article. The new report's heading: "Directions Home: Making Homelessness Rare, Short-Term, and Non-Recurring in Fort Worth, Texas, Within Ten Years." Its goals were ambitious but were set with the belief that they could actually be attained.[70]

The report's findings, upon which recommendations would be based, were both valuable and disturbing. They were cold but telling numbers. For instance, of the 1,700,000 Tarrant County residents, at least 4,042 were homeless at any point in time. Of this number, 16.5 percent were veterans, and almost one-third were children. More than half (52.7 percent) of the homeless suffered from conditions such as mental illness, substance abuse disorder, HIV infection, or physical disabilities that caused their homelessness or crippled their efforts to obtain and keep housing. And alarmingly, women and children who had become homeless after fleeing domestic violence comprised almost 20 percent of the homeless population. While granting that some progress had occurred in recent years, the report pointed to mounting evidence that the city's failure to provide sufficient resources to house disabled, long-term homeless people was costing the community dramatically in economic, social, and human terms. Claiming that this deplorable situation challenged Fort Worth's civic pride and moral sensibilities, the report contended, "It is time to end chronic homelessness and make other forms of homelessness rare, short-term, and non-recurring."[71]

At the heart of the commission's recommendations were several strategies to reach its ten-year goal. While all of these were important, the first three were critical: 1) Increase the supply of permanent supported housing, 2) Expand opportunities and services linked to accountability, and 3) Develop and operate a central resource facility. This third proposal envisioned an entity that, while not operating as an intake facility, would be a "one-stop" shop "where unsheltered and emergency-sheltered homeless residents can access critical services for stabilization, transition, assistance, and reintegration." In addition to these proposals, the commission recommended that a standing committee to deal with these matters remain intact and that transitional housing programs be scattered around Fort Worth instead of being concentrated in one area. The overall goal was ambitious—not merely manage homelessness, but end it.[72]

Union Gospel Mission had this same goal and was making large strides in that direction. Its financial success was fueling its efforts. Contributions in December 2008 exceeded the previous December by $50,000. And the direct-mail campaign was surpassing all expectations. The 2008 projected net income from these mailings was $534,192. The final tally was almost two-thirds higher—$875,567.[73]

While celebrated, the money was obviously not an end in itself but enabled the mission to create some innovative, needed programs. One of these, launched in 2008, provided primary health care to clients and guests of the mission. Called Healing Shepherd Clinic, it relieved overcrowded hospital emergency rooms and provided treatment for a number of conditions common to the homeless, such as heart, liver, and kidney disease; skin infections; pulmonary disease; diabetes; and hypertension. A volunteer physician, Dr. Alan Davenport, was named medical director.[74]

The plan called for Healing Shepherd Clinic to work closely with John Peter Smith Hospital to provide indigent patients, at no cost, prescription medications and diagnostic evaluations. But there was much more. Additional services would include complete physical examinations, treatment of chronic conditions, referrals for specialty care, and patient education and advocacy. During the months to come,

hundreds of patients would be seen and cared for.[75]

During those same months, the mission would meet a remarkable number of human needs. In many ways the numbers speak for themselves. In 2009, almost a half million meals were served. In the women's facilities an average of 282 beds were filled every night, and for men, a staggering 64,639 nights of safe shelter were provided—an average of 337 beds every night.[76]

These impressive numbers did not tell the whole story. There was more, especially in terms of opportunities for spiritual growth. Don Shisler had taken a big step in that direction in 2006 when he decided to seek a full-time chaplain. He knew the person he wanted—Episcopal priest Stanley Maneikis. Father Maneikis was familiar with the mission, having already given it much of his time. "I felt led to ask Stanley to do this," Don recalled. However, Stanley Maneikis was not so sure this was the path for him and prayed for God's guidance. Then one night, while in England, he prayed about it again and "it came to me," he said. "This is what I was to do."[77]

His decision made an immediate difference in the life of the mission. One of Father Maneikis's first steps was to launch the Alpha course—a biblically based, fifteen-lesson study series, led by trained volunteers. It soon became one of the foundation stones of a new spiritual growth emphasis at the mission. In 2009, 692 residents enrolled in Alpha classes, learning to apply biblical truths to their life situations. Six residents were baptized. "Our goal is to make Jesus Christ truly known, believed, and followed," said Father Maneikis. "I spend time with our residents. We pray together. We are committed to following God's lead ... as I pray each day, 'Dear Lord, don't let me get in the way of what you have planned.'"[78]

A resident named Dian was living testimony to this approach. Having experienced an abusive marriage and several addictions, then becoming homeless with almost no possessions, she finally landed at the mission. "Picture a brick wall," she said, "and you can't get past it. You need somebody to come with a chisel and then work on it a little every day and pretty soon, it comes down. That's what they do at Union Gospel Mission."[79]

She was not the only success. A young man who had developed a self-destructive lifestyle, alienated his family, and wound up living under a bridge said that before he found Union Gospel Mission of Tarrant County, "It didn't matter if I died or went to jail. I just didn't care. But people at the mission did," and the kind of care he received—spiritual, emotional, medical, educational, and physical—began transforming his life. He even enrolled in college courses. "Now I have a desire to live," he said. "I enjoy helping other people, and I plan to succeed. I know God loves me, has forgiven me, and will take care of me no matter what."[80]

The first weeks of 2010 were exceptionally cold, placing demands on a number of shelters. Union Gospel Mission of Tarrant County took as much of the area's overflow as possible and operated at maximum capacity—350 people. While handling these emergency needs, the mission also had other important, life-building issues to address. Children figured large here. Their problems were numerous and serious. Dr. George Curl, the mission's tutoring enrichment coordinator, explained: "A child falls behind in school by six months every time they move. Imagine the implications for a homeless child. Most we see are two or three years behind their grade level." To address this, the mission launched a Children's Enrichment Program that four nights a week brought children in for two hours of one-on-one tutoring with volunteers. Dr. Curl compared it to an extra day of school every week. "We're actually bringing kids up to grade level in six weeks. One student had never earned more than a C, but is now in hon-ors classes!" For young children, play therapy and childcare were also provided.[81]

In addition, medical care at the mission was improving and increasing. Four local hospitals had given a three-year grant to the Healing Shepherd Clinic. It had grown to three full-time staff members, eight volunteer doctors, and seven volunteer nurses. Working to improve the mental, physical, and spiritual well-being of their charges, by the end of 2010, they had provided full medical care for 1,500 patients and handled 1,328 office visits.[82]

It was not surprising that the needs of the homeless were growing, because Fort Worth's population was also burgeoning. In the short span of one decade, the city had grown more than 38 percent, the largest increase in eighty years. This meant more people on the street. Stanley Maneikis reported that more and more women were now in this situation; that, in fact, women were now representing the highest percentage of newly homeless people. And maybe even more surprising, homeless men with children, living under bridges and in makeshift camps, were increasing at an alarming rate.[83]

The president and board of Union Gospel Mission of Tarrant County chose to respond to these conditions. Discussions led to plans to build a large women's building on the campus, but not for women only. Several rooms would be set aside for homeless men with children. Schwarz-Hanson Architects were again put to work, and by March 2010, preliminary drawings of what was being called the new women's center were being prepared. They were soon shown to the board, and by May a conceptual design was completed. This ambitious venture was projected to be three stories and to cost at least $6,500,000. When estimates quickly exceeded that number, Don Shisler began announcing plans to raise $10 million and calling for prayers to support such an ambitious goal. By August the board was hearing that an increasing number of men with children were entering the mission and that more rooms for them were needed in the new facility. The project continued to grow until December, when plans for a forty-thousand-square-foot facility were unveiled.[84]

As 2010 drew to a close, the mission's staff could look back on a remarkable year. The numbers told an impressive story. Spiritual needs were being met with more than 1,600 chapel services and spiritual development programs for over 750 people. Basic needs were being met as never before. The mission had served 203,470 hot meals for men, women, and children; 25,200 sack lunches for those going to work or attending classes; 43,608 nights of safe shelter for women and children; and 62,890 nights of shelter for men struggling with addiction, poverty, and numerous life crises. Sixty-eight percent of the population were men, 23 percent women, and 9 percent were children under eighteen years old.[85]

The direct-mail initiative was one of the biggest programs making this progress possible. In February 2011, the mission board learned that total net revenue from direct mail was exceeding projections by $156,749, an increase of more than 20 percent. This effort was not only raising valuable income but also familiarizing a wide audience with the mission and investing new donors in its work.[86]

All these numbers, of course, were only a means to an end—helping people rebuild their lives. A lady named Kim learned this firsthand. Having grown up with an abusive, alcoholic father who encouraged her to drink and take drugs, Kim grew into a broken, dysfunctional adult who spent years, as she said, living "couch to couch." She became increasingly committed to reconciling with her fourteen-year-old son, who was living with his father, and getting clean from alcohol and drugs.

God's grace and guidance led her to Union Gospel Mission of Tarrant County. It was a lifesaver. "I'm just doing everything I need to do to better my life," she said. "I've already got a job." She was waiting tables but, in addition, was preparing daily meals at the mission. Finding real fulfillment in this, she said, "I don't want to leave the kitchen." She was giving more than food. She was giving herself. "When you give the guests a good meal, they really know you love them, if you put your heart in it. I tell them to have a blessed day. . . . When I'm out on the streets, they know me as the kitchen lady."[87]

Kim was not naïve. She knew there was hard work ahead to build a stable life and reconcile with her son. But she also knew something else: "Nobody said following the Cross was going to be easy. But God has always been there. You've got to keep your head up and keep on moving and He's there for you."[88]

# CHAPTER NINE

Today, to help Kim and many others, Union Gospel Mission of Tarrant County no longer tries to handle complicated life issues alone. It works with thirty-two diverse social service organizations to assist residents with life guidance and to help them gain independence. Bus passes and even private transportation are made available to the Recovery Resource Council, which provides life-skills classes and referrals for substance abuse treatments. A number of agencies come to the mission to provide their services. Mental Health Mental Retardation visits once a week to assess residents with mental health issues and assist them in getting services in the appropriate MHMR clinic. The Parenting Center and Cook Children's Behavioral Health Services staff conduct parenting classes for residents in the Family Center. Lena Pope Home provides on-site play therapy weekly. SafeHaven of Tarrant County offers domestic violence counseling. There are many more resources, including even Tarrant County Food Bank's Cooking Matters class, which teaches cooking basics to residents who are about to leave and begin new lives.[1]

If there is such a thing as a typical day in the life of a mother with children at the mission, it begins with breakfast at 5:30 a.m. and a 6:30 a.m. mission bus picking up children attending day care. At 7:00, the bus returns to load up the school-age children. The mothers then begin their daily routine of laundry, learning, and housekeeping chores. They are also responsible for maintaining the entire floor where they live. At 9:00 they meet with case managers to review their individual service plans, identifying priorities, goals, strategies, and resources to maximize their well-being. By 10:30 they are attending Life Skill classes, focusing on how to keep a job and work as a team, how to manage money and time, and how to communicate effectively. After an 11:30 lunch they participate in a number of groups such as counseling, domestic violence counseling, GED classes, college courses, employment training, nutrition, and financial literacy. Later in the day, with children home from school, residents participate in a chapel service, and since many of the children are behind in school, they attend tutoring classes while their mothers are in parenting sessions. On Thursday afternoons, mothers also participate in the Alpha spiritual development program, an opportunity to study the Bible, draw closer to Jesus Christ, and grow spiritually. By 8:00 p.m. children are heading to bed as their mothers prepare for another day in their journeys toward healing.[2]

Union Gospel Mission of Tarrant County has grown and matured in ways that few could have predicted. It now partners with thirty-two social-service organizations to provide a wide range of services to the homeless. Ten of these agencies actually come to the mission to offer help. Almost two hundred men and women, as well as thirty families, complete the mission's program annually and return to society. Because of the mission's tutoring program, most of their children also experience marked in-

PROPOSED WOMEN'S DORMITORY
UNION GOSPEL MISSION OF TARRANT COUNTY
FORT WORTH, TEXAS

Architectural rendering of the Scott Walker
Women and Families Service Building.
Union Gospel Mission of Tarrant County collection.

creases in reading and math scores.[3]

The mission is served today by a large number of invaluable volunteers. The mission partners with some sixty churches, which provide most of the seven hundred-plus people giving thousands of hours annually to the mission's work. They do everything from helping in the kitchen, tutoring, and sorting items in the warehouse to leading chapel services, gardening, and hosting special events. Father Maneikis has played a large role in making all this happen. He has strengthened ties with these partner churches, and under his leadership, the Alpha class has ministered to nearly seven hundred residents a year.[4]

Today, a walk along the thirteen- and four-

teen-hundred blocks of East Lancaster is an immersion into a world of the homeless and those trying desperately to survive. Within the shadow of Fort Worth's booming downtown and new urban-housing initiatives are people shuffling along, sacks under their arms and trash bags over their shoulders, easily overlooked by people busy with their own daily lives. Some, having slept on streets and under bridges, sit on curbs; others, weary, stretch out on blankets that do little to soften the pavement beneath them.

In the midst of this setting of little hope and big need is Union Gospel Mission of Tarrant County. Although celebrating its 125th birthday, it is not showing its age. In fact, it seems younger and newer than ever. It is meeting more and more needs every year and helping rebuild broken lives. Fundraising is in high gear for a new women and families service building, which will have a transforming impact on the mission's ability to serve "the least of these." With women comprising 28 percent of the homeless population in Tarrant County, and with the mission receiving more than twenty calls a day from women wanting to enroll in its program, this new facility will help address numerous needs. It will have twenty-eight rooms for single women (double occupancy), twelve overnight-shelter beds for women, and five rooms for families with children. To help deal with the growing number of homeless fathers, five rooms will be devoted to homeless men with children. This new addition, the Scott Walker Women and Families Service Building, is scheduled to open in the first quarter of 2016. It will also offer offices for program directors, a library and computer room, a commercial-size laundry, a chapel, prayer room, hair salon, courtyard, and a large activity room.[5]

Funding has also been a remarkable story. In 1999, the mission's operating budget was $1,300,000. By 2012, it had risen to $4,350,000. The direct-mail campaign initiated in 2003 has dramatically impacted these numbers. More than 11,500 people regularly support the mission. Since 1999, more than $27,000,000 has been received for operating revenue and almost $19,000,000 for capital projects, amounts that just a few years ago would have seemed impossible.[6]

What changes have happened with the mission since Charley Byron, heading for his vaudeville act, stepped inside to see what this place was! It was not much then—just a day-to-day outpost doing its best to help cowboys, prostitutes, drunks, and drifters in a booming frontier town. It is still helping people, but in ways and on a scale that Charley Byron could not have imagined. With a budget exceeding $4,800,000, with facilities among the best in the nation and skilled personnel to deal with many difficult life issues, with generous donors and record numbers of volunteers, Union Gospel Mission of Tarrant County can both value its rich past and look forward to an ever-expanding, service-filled future.

# POSTSCRIPT

The story of Union Gospel Mission of Tarrant County is really the story of God at work in and among the people who walk through its doors. It is that foundation of faith that propels its residents into new opportunities for growth, healing, and change that can help them leave its doors as independent and productive members of our city. With its unique calling to end homelessness one person at a time, Union Gospel Mission of Tarrant County continues to seek new avenues for partnership in Fort Worth and Tarrant County.

In the secure environment of Union Gospel Mission of Tarrant County's six-acre campus, residents participate in a holistic approach taken to address physical, mental, emotional, social, and spiritual needs. UGM-TC provides space in which a person can openly discuss his or her unique situation, needs, concerns, strengths, and hopes. The programs offered aim to give homeless individuals the greatest chance to develop the skills and self-confidence necessary to attain self-sufficiency. Upon a client's entry into the program, a professional social worker conducts a face-to-face comprehensive assessment with that individual. Together, they identify the client's strengths and challenges while establishing a trusting and empowering relationship. This is done through a case-management plan designed to address the overall needs of each client.

Today, Union Gospel Mission of Tarrant County partners with over thirty-two diverse social service organizations that provide guidance to help residents move toward independence. Residents are placed into specific programs for men, women, and families provided by these organizations as well as by UGM-TC. Each year two hundred men and women and thirty families complete these programs and return to society. Children are given new study- and life-skills, while moms and dads develop new parenting skills with commitments to follow through and become healthy families. Emergency services include meals and overnight shelter for men.

The skill-building program focuses on improving residents' personal and social behaviors to increase their chances of keeping meaningful relationships and productive employment. The program is designed to build character by teaching and modeling responsible and dependable behaviors and values that increase self-confidence, build self-esteem, create healthy relationships, and improve social skills.

Homeless people report that they feel alone in the world because they do not have supportive relationships with family or friends. Studies have demonstrated that having a network of caring relationships contributes to physiological well-being. Residents begin to build a social network through the programs offered at UGM-TC. As residents participate in life skills, anger management, and domestic violence education classes, they begin to regain a sense of self-worth and redevelop their social skills.

UGM-TC is committed to the spiritual development of each individual as a key component in changing the lives of the homeless population. Active participation in a community of faith can give residents a sense of connection and belonging. UGM-TC offers daily worship services and a comprehensive religious education program. The daily chapel services offer a true sanctuary in the peaceful Deborah Hall Chapel for residents and guests from the street. Thursdays at the mission are planned as spiritual development days for residents, utilizing the Alpha USA curriculum. Alpha allows individuals to experience a loving God as they move into a relationship with Jesus Christ. The curriculum incorporates praise and worship, video teachings, and small groups where residents can discuss their thoughts more intimately with staff and trained Alpha leaders.

In the time that children live at UGM-TC, the Children's Enrichment Program gives them the basic skills and tools they need to do well in school and to move forward in their lives. Year-round, the program provides a safe, consistent, and fun place to learn.

Homeless children often enter school and society with low self-image and lack of social skills, which contribute to ongoing difficulties in the classroom with peers. Chaotic or non-existing homes, lack of discipline, and spotty attendance also create barriers to children's learning.

Once children are accommodated at UGM-TC, they are enrolled into the Children's Enrichment Program. Each child is required to attend tutoring Monday through Thursday for two hours each evening. This program focuses on finding and establishing the child's strengths and weaknesses. Once these are identified, a personal plan of action will be developed to overcome the child's educational obstacles.

The Healing Shepherd Clinic provides primary care to the residents of UGM-TC. The homeless are exposed to harsh weather, malnutrition, diseases, and lack of sanita-

tion. Many are unaware that they have chronic health conditions like diabetes, heart disease, or mental illness. Often, their only option for medical care is to go to the emergency room. The Healing Shepherd Clinic provides primary and preventive care to the residents of UGM-TC. Patients at the clinic can be treated for the many common illnesses and conditions that are prevalent in the homeless population including heart, liver, and kidney diseases; skin infections; chronic pulmonary disease; diabetes; and hypertension.

Volunteer physicians donate their time each week to treat patients, assisted by a full-time nurse practitioner and volunteer RNs and medical assistants. Together, they care for the mental, physical, and spiritual well-being of residents and guests. Healing Shepherd Clinic is a separate 501(c)(3) non-profit operating on the campus of Union Gospel Mission of Tarrant County.

The Warehouse serves as the donation center for UGM-TC. It then serves individuals who are currently homeless by providing them with clothing and toiletries. Once a resident successfully completes the program, UGM-TC does its best to provide the essentials they need to live independently. With a referral from a partner agency, individuals currently getting out of homelessness or poverty can utilize the Warehouse for household items such as furniture and appliances. All of this is made possible thanks to donations from community supporters.

Throughout its history, volunteers have been vitally important to Union Gospel Mission of Tarrant County. The mission associates with some sixty churches that provide most of the more than seven hundred people offering thousands of hours annually to aid its work. Volunteer support includes time spent in the kitchen, tutoring and working with children, sorting items in the Warehouse, leading chapel services, gardening, teaching Bible studies, and hosting special events, among countless other activities. This volunteer support from the community has been critical to expanding ministry and services through the mission and will be even more important to its work in the future.

Unique among agencies, UGM-TC is privately funded, committed to representing its donors' stewardship of time and gifts with careful management and sound business practice. Union Gospel Mission of Tarrant County is a member of the Association of Gospel Rescue Missions (AGRM). It is a charity accredited by the Better Business Bureau (BBB) and highly rated on both Charity Navigator and GuideStar, and it participates in Commitment to Transparency. UGM-TC adheres to the highest standards of Christian stewardship and ethical financial practices.

In recent years, UGM-TC has poured a remarkable 81 percent of its financial resources directly into programs and services, with just 19 percent of its annual budget utilized to support its operating expenses. Funding for the mission continues to flow largely from individuals who provide 79 percent of its annual budget. Foundations, trusts, and business give just over 17 percent, with churches contributing an additional 4 percent. The generosity of these wonderful partners will continue to expand the work of the mission in the years ahead. It is the critical link in ministering to its residents and fulfilling its mission.

Union Gospel Mission of Tarrant County continues its quest to end homelessness with a commitment to faith and work in our community. The campus continues to expand with new buildings to house women and family services. Future new initiatives include additional housing, retail partners, and other social services partners to bolster the already strong services in the Lancaster corridor. Never has the mission's commitment been stronger to innovate and dream to change the lives of its residents in Fort Worth. And never has the need been greater.

It is a bold task to commit to ending homelessness. Union Gospel Mission of Tarrant County is more firmly committed to this mission today than ever. The words of Jesus resound through every facet of its work: "Come to me, all who are weary and heavy-laden, and you will find rest for your souls." UGM-TC opens its doors to the weary and heavy-laden, welcoming people as children coming home. And when they leave these same doors, they do so as independent people with new life skills and the faith to move forward into exciting, new, and productive lives. That is the history of Union Gospel Mission of Tarrant County, and that is its future: God's healthy place, ending homelessness one person at a time.

# NOTES

## Introduction

1. *City Voices*, Summer, 1995.
2. Arthur Bonner, *Enacted Christianity: Evangelical Rescue Missions in the United States and Canada* (Bloomington, Indiana: XLibris Corporation, 2002), 35, 40-41.
3. Ibid. pp. 42-47; William E. Paul, *The Romance of Rescue* (Minneapolis: Osterhus Publishing House, 1946), 21-28.
4. Bonner, 47; Paul, 26-27.
5. Bonner, 47-51; Steve Berger, interview with author, June 16, 2006.
6. Paul, 14-16.
7. Sidney E. Ahlstrom, *A Religious History of the American People* (New Haven and London: Yale University Press, 1972), 812-819.

## Chapter 1

1. Oliver Knight, *Fort Worth: Outpost on the Trinity* (Norman: University of Oklahoma Press, 1953), pp. 154-156; *Directory of the City of Fort Worth, 1888-89* (Galveston, Texas: Morrison & Fourney), pp. 45 ff.
2. Knight, pp. 129-136; Richard E. Selcer, *Hell's Half Acre: The Life and Legend of a Red-Light District* (Fort Worth: Texas Christian University Press, 1991), pp. 216-219; *Fort Worth Democrat*, 4/19/1873; Research Data, Fort Worth Public Library, 1083, 1084.
3. *Directory of the City of Fort Worth*, p. 46; *Fort Worth Monthly Bulletin* (Fort Worth: Young Men's Christian Association, March, 1891), p. 6.
4. Interview with The Rt. Reverend Sam B. Hulsey, January 26, 2006. Retired Bishop Hulsey is a grandson of Charley Byron.
5. Hulsey interview; Ahlstrom, pp. 743-745.
6. *Fort Worth Monthly Bulletin*, p. 6; *Dallas Morning News*, February 15, 1894. Hereafter referred to as *DMN*.
7. *DMN*, March 26, 1893, March 29, 1893.
8. Ibid.
9. Ibid.
10. Ibid.
11. Ibid.
12. *DMN*, February 7, 1894.
13. *DMN*, February 15, 1894.
14. *DMN*, 2/26/1894.
15. *DMN*, 4/6/1894.
16. *DMN*, 10/8/1894, 10/16/1894, 3/9/1896.
17. *Fort Worth Record*, 1/5/1897. Hereafter referred to as *FWR*.
18. *FWR*, 2/13/1897.
19. *FWR*, 3/11/1897, 3/12/1897, 3/14/1897, 5/18/1897.
20. *FWR*, 8/15/1897, 10/12/1897.
21. *FW Register*, 3/3/1897.
22. *FWR*, 7/9/1897, 9/30/1897.
23. *FWR*, 10/10/1897, 10/17/1897.

## Chapter 2

1. Hulsey interview; song provided by Hulsey.
2. *Fort Worth Star-Telegram*, 6/28/1925. Hereafter referred to as *FWST*.
3. Edward Henry Manwarring, *A Brief History of Union Gospel Mission* (Master of Theology thesis, Southwestern Baptist Theological Seminary, Fort Worth, Texas, 1928, p. 4). Hereafter referred to as *EHM*.
4. Ibid. p. 8.
5. Ibid. p. 13.
6. *DMN*, 3/6/1906; *FWST* 9/16/1921.
7. *Fort Worth Press*, 12—21 (date unknown); Leslie Green interview.
8. *FWST* 1/2/1916.
9. Ibid.
10. Ibid.
11. *FWST*, 2/2/1916 and 2/11/1916.
12. *FWST* 2/3/1916 and 2/6/1916.
13. *FWST* 2/24/1916.
14. Zlatkovich, Charles P., *Texas & Pacific Railway: Operations and Traffic*, Westover Press, El Paso, Texas, 1998, p. 3.
15. *FWST*, 3/26/1916.
16. *FWST*, 2/15/1916.
17. Ibid.
18. *FWST*, 4/9/1916.
19. *FWST*, 5/21/1916.
20. *FWST*, 5/21/1916; *DMN* 5/21/1916.

21. *DMN*, 5/21/1916; *FWST*, 5/21/1916.
22. *FWST*, 11/16/1916.
23. *FWST*, 4/11/1917, p. 2; 4/13/1917, p. 1; 4/17/1917, p. 1.

## Chapter 3

1. *DMN*, 10/17/1917, 10/22/1917.
2. *DMN*, 12/17/1917.
3. *DMN*, 2/8/1918.
4. *DMN*, 2/8/1918, 2/18/1918, 8/19/1918.
5. *DMN*, 2/18/1918, 7/1/1918, 7/29/1918.
6. *DMN*, 8/19/1918, 8/25/1918.
7. *EHM*, p. 11.
8. *DMN*, 9/19/1919.
9. *DMN*, 9/29/1919, 10/16/1919, 11/24/1919.
10. *DMN*, 1/19/1920.
11. *DMN*, 9/6/1920.
12. *DMN*, 9/12/1921.
13. *FWST*, 9/16/1921.
14. *DMN*, 11/7/1921, 11/21/1921.
15. *DMN*, 11/28/1921.
16. *DMN*, 4/11/1922.
17. *DMN*, 1/2/1922.
18. *DMN*, 1/9/1922.
19. *FWST*, 1/25/1922.
20. *FWST*, 2/9/1922; DMN 2/10/1922.
21. *FWST*, 3/2/1922; *DMN*, 3/3/1922.
22. *FWST*, 3/8/1922.
23. *FWST*, 3/21/1922.
24. *DMN*, 3/29/1922; FWST 4/1/1922.
25. *DMN*, 5/29/1922.
26. *DMN*, 6/5/1922; FWST 6/15/1922.
27. *DMN*, 7/2/1922; FWST, 7/4/1922.
28. *FWST*, 10/9/1922, 10/11/1922.
29. *FWST*, 12/11/1922.
30. *FWST*, 12/23/1922.
31. *FWST*, 12/26/1922.
32. *DMN*, 2/21/1923.
33. *DMN*, 5/28/1923, 6/4/1923, 6/11/1923.
34. *FWST*, 6/25/1923.
35. Ibid.
36. *FWST*, 6/26/1923.
37. *DMN*, 7/16/1923.
38. *DMN*, 8/20/1923, 8/27/1923, 9/17/1923.
39. *DMN*, 5/6/1925, 11/1/1927.
40. *DMN*, 6/29/1925.
41. *EHM*, pp. 15-16.
42. *Fort Worth Press* 2/5/1926; *FWST* 2/5/1926.
43. *DMN*, 4/27/1926, 7/11/1926, 11/1/1927; *Union Gospel Mission of Tarrant County, 40th Annual Report, 1929*.
44. *FWST*, 10/10/1926.
45. Ibid.

46. Ibid.
47. Ibid.
48. Ibid.
49. Ibid.
50. *Union Gospel Mission of Tarrant County, Fortieth Annual Report* (for 1928).
51. *Fortieth Annual Report*, p. 6; *Record Telegram*, 7/22/1929.
52. *FWST*, 6/2/1929.
53. Perkins, Dexter and Van Deusen, Glyndon G. *The United States of America: A History, Since 1865*. Macmillan Co., New York, 1968, pp. 493, 496-497.

## Chapter 4

1. "The New Frontier," p. 58.
2. Knight, p. 210.
3. John B. Collier, Jr., was the new vice president, Max Bergman, chairman of finance. *FW Record Telegram*, 1/25/1930; *DMN*, 1/24/1930, 5/3/1930, 5/4/1930, 5/5/1930.
4. *DMN*, 5/4/1930, 5/5/1930, 5/6/1930.
5. *DMN*, 5/7/1930.
6. *FWST*, 10/16/2005.
7. Ibid.
8. *DMN*, 10/16/1934.
9. *FWST*, 1/5/1935, 2/11/1935.
10. *FWST*, 4/2/1935.
11. *FWST*, 4/2/1935, 7/23/1935.
12. *DMN*, 10/1/1935.
13. *FWST*, 1/14/1936.
14. *FWST*, 3/1/1936.
15. *FWST*, 10/8/1936, 1/26/1937.
16. *FWST*, 1/26/1937.
17. *DMN*, 9/28/1937.
18. *FWST*, 1/16/1938, 1/17/1938; *DMN* 1/18/1938.
19. *FWST*, 1/17/1938.

## Chapter 5

1. Written statement provided by Leslie Green, 2/11/2007.
2. Interview with Leslie Green, 2/11/2007.
3. *FWST*, 10/11/1938.
4. Green written statement, 2/11/2007.
5. *FWST*, 10/29/1939.
6. Ibid.
7. *FWST*, 6/15/1941.
8. *FWST*, 9/6/1941; statement by Shannon Shipp, Texas Christian University, 9/16/2008.
9. *FWST*, 11/4/1941; Shipp statement, 9/16/2008.
10. *FWST*, 8/20/1942.
11. Green interview, 2/11/2007.

12. Written statement provided by Leslie Green, 2006.
13. Ibid.
14. Ibid.
15. Ibid.
16. Leslie Green, interview with author, 6/15/2006.
17. Ibid.
18. *FWST*, 11/17/1943; Green interview 2/11/2007.
19. Green interview, 6/15/2006.
20. Green interview, 2/11/2007.
21. *FWST*, 12/30/1947.
22. Ibid.
23. *DMN*, 9/14/1994.
24. *DMN*, 9/14/1994; interview with Terry Smith, 3/1/2006.
25. Perkins, Kent. "Tuesday Night in Texas."
26. Smith interview, 3/1/2006.
27. *Fort Worth Press*, 1/21/1962, hereafter *FWP*.
28. Ibid.
29. Ewell Humphrey interview, 12/1/2005.
30. Ibid.
31. Ibid.
32. Ibid.
33. Ibid.
34. *FWP*, 2/10/1965; *DMN*, 2/11/1965.
35. *FWP*, 2/10/1965.
36. *FWP*, 3/29/1965.
37. Ibid.
38. *FWST*, 12/24/1965.
39. *FWST*, 12/25/1965.
40. UGM-TC letter, November, 1966.
41. Ibid.
42. UGM-TC letter, December, 1966.
43. Ibid.
44. UGM-TC letter, February, 1967.
45. Ibid.
46. Ibid.
47. Ibid.
48. Ibid.
49. *FWP*, 12/12/1967.
50. Ibid.
51. *UGM-TC Newsletter*, 1968.
52. *UGM-TC Newsletter*, 1969.
53. *UGM-TC Newsletter*, winter, 1970.
54. *FWST*, 4/25/1970.
55. Interview with Bill Russell, 6/5/2005.
56. Interview with Tom Redwine, 11/15/2005; *DMN* 3/16/1978; *FWST* 3/16/1978; interview with Otis Lemley, 5/1/2006.
57. *FWST*, 8/27/1978.
58. *Union Gospel Mission of Tarrant County Newsletter*, 1974.
59. Ibid.
60. Ibid.
61. Ibid.
62. Ibid.
63. Ibid.
64. Ibid.
65. Ibid.

**Chapter 6**

1. *Union Gospel Mission of Tarrant County Newsletter*, 1974.
2. Ibid.
3. *FWST*, 12/25/1974.
4. Ibid.
5. Ibid.
6. Ibid.
7. Ibid.
8. Ibid.
9. Ibid.
10. *DMN*, 4/27/1975.
11. *FWST*, 8/27/1978.
12. *DMN*, 3/16/1978.
13. *DMN*, 3/16/1978.
14. Ibid.
15. *DMN*, 3/16/1978.
16. Ibid.

**Chapter 7**

1. FWST, 8/27/1978.
2. Ibid.
3. Ibid.
4. Ibid.
5. Interview with Columba Reid, 2/15/2006.
6. *FWST*, 8/27/1978.
7. Reid interview, 2/15/2006; *FWST*, 8/27/1978.
8. *FWST*, 8/27/1978.
9. Ibid.
10. Interview with Betty Hedgepeth, 3/23/2006, 2/24/2009.
11. Interview with Tom Redwine, 7/23/2008.
12. Redwine interview, 7/23/2008.
13. "What Is Union Gospel Mission?" Bob Scott, 1981,
14. Ibid.
15. Ibid.
16. Ibid.
17. *FWST*, 11/23/1983.
18. Ibid.
19. Ibid.
20. Ibid.
21. *Union Gospel Light*, January 1984.
22. Ibid.
23. *Union Gospel Light*, April 1984.

24. *Union Gospel Light*, August 1984.
25. Ibid.
26. Ibid.
27. *Union Gospel Light*, February 1985.
28. *FWST*, 12/6/1984.
29. *Union Gospel Light*, May 1987.
30. *Union Gospel Light*, August 1987.
31. *Union Gospel Light*, September 1987.
32. *Union Gospel Light*, January 1987.
33. *Union Gospel Light*, November 1988, April 1989.
34. *Union Gospel Light*, February 1989.
35. Ibid.
36. Ibid.
37. *Union Gospel Light*, April 1989.
38. *FWST*, 1/3/1989.
39. Ibid.
40. Ibid.
41. Ibid.
42. Ibid.
43. Ibid.
44. *Union Gospel Light*, February 1990.
45. *Union Gospel Light*, March-April 1990.
46. Ibid; *Union Gospel Light*, April 1991.
47. *FWST*, 12/19/1993; interview with Don Webb, 2/20/2006.
48. Webb interview, 2/20/2006.
49. Ibid.
50. Ibid.
51. *Union Gospel Light*, September 1990.
52. Ibid.
53. Ibid.
54. *Union Gospel Light*, April 1991.
55. Ibid.
56. *Union Gospel Light*, April 1991.
57. *FWST*, 7/29/1992.
58. Ibid.
59. Ibid.
60. Ibid.
61. *FWST*, 11/17/1992.
62. Ibid; *FWST*, November 1992; *Union Gospel Light*, April 1992.
63. Ibid.
64. Ibid.; *FWST*, no date.
65. *FWST*, 3/1/1993, 3/2/1993.
66. *FWST*, 11/17/1992, 10/23/1993.
67. *FWST*, 11/27/1993.
68. *FWST*, 12/19/1993.
69. *FWST*, 5/1/1994.
70. Ibid.
71. Ibid.
72. *FWST*, 11/6/1994.

73. *FWST*, 11/6/1994, interview with David Conner, 2/28/2006.
74. Conner interview, 2/28/2006, 1/27/2011.
75. *FWST*, 11/6/1994.

**Chapter 8**
1. Don Shisler interview, 10/6/2010.
2. Ibid.
3. Ibid.
4. Shisler interview, 5/10/2011.
5. *Union Gosper Mission of Tarrant County Annual Report*, 1985; Shisler interview, 5/10/2011; Conner interview, 1/27/2011.
6. Shisler interview, 5/10/2011.
7. Ibid.
8. Ibid.
9. Shisler interview, 5/20/2011.
10. Shisler interview, 5/20/2011. Frenchy eventually got cancer, was moved to a nursing home, and from there to a hospital, where he died. His ex-wife, Danielle's mother, was a street person who cycled in and out of shelters. She got custody of Danielle, a development that quickly turned bad. Danielle was then adopted by a black minister and finally began to have a healthy, positive life. In recent years she has made periodic contact with Union Gospel Mission, thankful for its helpful role in her life.
11. Shisler interview, 5/10/2011.
12. *Union Gospel Mission of Tarrant County Annual Report*, 1995, p. 7.
13. Ibid.
14. Ibid. p. 9.
15. Ibid. p. 9.
16. *FWST*, 12-30-1995; *Union Gospel Mission of Tarrant County Annual Report*, 11 1995, p.5.
17. *FWST*, 3-16-1997.
18. Shisler interview, 5/10/2011; Conner interview, 3/23/2006.
19. Shisler interview, 5/20/2011.
20. *FWST*, 6/8/1997.
21. Ibid.
22. Ibid.
23. Ibid.
24. Ibid.
25. Ibid.
26. Ibid.
27. Ibid.
28. Ibid.
29. *Directions Home: Making Homelessness Rare, Short-Term and Non-Recurring in Fort Worth, Texas Within Ten Years*, Mayor's Advisory Commission on Home-

lessness, Summer, 2008. Hereafter referred to as Mayor's Commission on Homelessness.

30. *FWST*, 11/5/1997; Shisler interview, 5/20/2011.

31. Larry Eason interview, 5/18/2011.

32. Ibid.

33. Eason interview, 6/29/2011.

34. Eason interview 6/29/2011; UGM-TC Board Of Directors retreat, 9/26/1998.

35. UGM-TC board retreat, 9/26/1998.

36. *Union Gospel Mission of Tarrant County Strategic Plan*.

37. Ibid.

38. Eason interview, 6/29/2011; board minutes 3/25/1999, 9/16/1999, 10/21/1999.

39. *FWST*, 2/4/2001; Eason interview, 5/18/2011; board minutes 12/16/1999.

40. Board minutes 1/2000, 3/23/2000, 4/20/2000, 6/15/2000.

41. Board minutes, 1/11/2001; Eason interview, 6/20/2011.

42. "What Will It Take to End Homelessness?" Urban Institute, Washington, DC, September 2001.

43. Board minutes 3/27/2003, 4/17/2003, 9/18/2003; Eason interview, 6/20/2011.

44. "Religion for Today," Direct Mailing, December 2003.

45. *FWST*, 12/26/2003.

46. Ibid.

47. Ibid.

48. Board minutes, 3/11/2004, 10/21/2004; Eason interview, 6/29/2011.

49. Eason interview 6/29/2011; board minutes 3/11/2004, 5/13/2004, 10/21/2004, 12/16/2004.

50. *FWST*, 3/28/2004.

51. Board minutes, 12/16/2004; *Union Gospel Mission of Tarrant County, 2004 Annual Report*.

52. *Union Gospel Mission of Tarrant County, 2004 Annual Report*.

53. Ibid.

54. Ibid.

55. Ibid.

56. Ibid.

57. Board minutes 4/21/2005; the *Mission*, Union Gospel Mission of Tarrant County, Fall 2005.

58. The *Mission*, Union Gospel Mission of Tarrant County, Fall 2005.

59. Ibid.

60. Ibid.

61. Schwarz-Hanson Architects, *Analysis of Development Options for UGM-TC Men's Facilities*, 3/24/2006; Memo of Understanding Between Union Gospel Mission of Tarrant County and Paulos Properties,

September 2006.

62. Ron Hall and Denver Moore: *Same Kind of Different as Me* (Nashville: CCW Publishing House, 2006).

63. Shisler interview, 5/20/2011.

64. National Alliance to End Homelessness, *Chronic Homelessness: Federal Policy Brief*. Washington, DC, March 12, 2007.

65. Ibid.

66. Ibid.

67. *FWST*, 1/27/2007.

68. Ibid.

69. Ibid.

70. Eason interview, 6/29/2011; Mayor's Commission on Homelessness.

71. Mayor's Commission on Homelessness, pp. 9, 13.

72. Ibid. pp. 19, 37–39; *FWST*, 2008.

73. Board minutes, 1/15/2009, 4/16/2009.

74. "God's Healthy Place: The Healing Shepherd Clinic," Union Gospel Mission, n.d.

75. Ibid.; board minutes, 2/19/2009.

76. *Union Gospel Mission of Tarrant County 2009 Annual Report*.

77. Father Stanley Maneikis interview, 5/20/2011.

78. *Union Gospel Mission of Tarrant County 2009 Annual Report*; Maneikis interview, 5/20/2011.

79. *Union Gospel Mission of Tarrant County 2009 Annual Report*.

80. *Union Gospel Mission of Tarrant County 2010 Annual Report*, p. 6.

81. Board minutes, 2/18/2010; *2010 Annual Report*, pp. 8–9.

82. *2010 Annual Report*.

83. *FWST* 2/18/2011; board minutes, 5/20/2011; Shisler interview, 5/20/2011.

84. Board minutes, 3/25/2010, 4/15/2010, 5/20/2010, 8/19/2010, 11/18/2010, 12/16/2012.

85. *2010 Annual Report*.

86. Board minutes, 2/17/2011.

87. *The Mission*, Fall 2011.

88. Ibid.

## Chapter 9

1. "God's Healthy Place: Partnered Social Service Agencies," UGM, n.d.

2. "A Day In The Life Of…" UGM, n.d.

3. Larry Eason paper, 10/2/2012.

4. Ibid; Union Gospel Mission of Tarrant County, *2012 Volunteer Manual*.

5. UGM Campaign packet, 2012.

6. Eason paper, 10/2/2012.

# INDEX